Picture the Past
# THE PEAK DISTRICT

# Picture the Past
# THE PEAK DISTRICT

Neil Bettridge

# ACKNOWLEDGEMENTS

The editor would like to thank his colleagues at the Local Studies Library, County Hall Matlock for their help and encouragement, in particular Susan Hulse and Catherine Moorcroft for editorial assistance and Yvonne Chalker of Buxton Library for help in sourcing images. Particular thanks are due to many kind individuals and organisations for permission to reproduce images.

Those who wished to be named are credited alongside their images. Others have preferred to remain anonymous. Unfortunately some photographs were given to the library so long ago that it has been impossible to trace the donors. Any such donors are earnestly requested to contact the Local Studes Library.

First published in Great Britain in 2008 by The Breedon Books Publishing Company Limited, Breedon House, 3 The Parker Centre, Derby, DE21 4SZ.

This paperback edition published in Great Britain in 2014 by DB Publishing, an imprint of JMD Media Ltd

ISBN 978-1-78091-426-8

Printed and bound in the UK by Copytech (UK) Ltd Peterborough

# CONTENTS

# INTRODUCTION

In the past, anyone wanting to view the collections of hundreds of thousands of old images in the libraries and museums of Derbyshire or Nottinghamshire would have had to travel many miles to try and track down the ones they were interested in. This proved to be frustrating and time consuming for researchers, a barrier to anyone from further afield and damaging to the more fragile images from all the handling. The collections include photographs, slides, negatives, glass plates, postcards and engravings recalling the history of our local communities for a hundred years and more.

Thankfully senior staff in four local authorities got their heads together to solve the problem and the idea of conserving the images using digitisation, while at the same time giving people all over the world access to the digitised versions, was conceived.

Funding was obtained from the Heritage Lottery Fund at the beginning of 2002 together with additional cash from the four partner authorities, Derbyshire and Nottinghamshire County Councils and the City Councils of Derby and Nottingham. Local studies staff in the libraries and museums started collating images and information ready for inclusion in the project and sent out thousands of letters requesting copyright clearance from the original photographers or their relatives. Nick Tomlinson was appointed as project manager to lead a team of experienced professionals inputting the information into a custom-built database and carefully digitising the images.

The Picture the Past website (www.picturethepast.org.uk) was launched in June 2003 and by the end of 2007 in excess of 67,000 pictures had been added. It now attracts well over 10,000 visitors from all over the world viewing thousands of pages of images every month. The site is updated on a regular basis and actually gives the user the ability to 'correct' existing information or add more information to those pictures with scant details.

The website is designed to be as 'easy to use' as possible and includes a simple keyword search facility as well as more comprehensive search mechanisms for users looking for images with a particular theme or by a specific photographer. Visitors can print out low resolution copies for their own personal use or study purposes but for those users wanting to own a top quality glossy photographic copy the website includes an online ordering service. Thanks to the involvement of *Derby Evening Telegraph* this enables users to browse the collection and order and pay for their selections securely online. The prints are produced on state-of-the-art equipment and, as a non-profit making project, all the income raised from this service goes back into the conservation and preservation of more original pictures.

This book gives you the chance to sample just a handful of the images contained in the website and it is very much hoped that you will go on to enjoy the rest of the pictures online.

For people who do not have access to the Internet at home, or who are not sure where to start, there are computers available for public use in all libraries and the local studies staff are more than willing to help you get started.

## The website can be viewed at www.picturethepast.org.uk

Nick Tomlinson and Robert Gent receiving the SOCITM award in 2007

### Picture Website Wins National Accolades

Picture the Past' continues to go from strength to strength by winning an award in the 2007 Local Government IT Excellence Awards.

The awards, which are organised by Intellect, SOCITM and SOLACE and sponsored by Ericom, highlight the use of best practice in local government and how IT has been used both effectively and innovatively to deliver best-value public services. The judges were impressed with both the originality of the solution, and its potential for expansion and emulation, and they commended the project team's commitment to utilise technology in order to preserve the region's heritage. The website won the Alan Ball Local History Award in 2004 in recognition of its commitment to local history publishing.

The awards are made every year by the Library Services Trust to public libraries and local authorities who – through books, magazines, websites or any other form of the written word – promote their communities' local history.

Michael Saich, Chairman of the Library Services Trust, presented the award on 19 January 2005. He remarked 'Picture the Past was successful in competition with both print and non-print entries in gaining one of the main awards. The Trust was impressed by how successfully the partners worked together to create the website and we feel it is important for local authorities to continue to produce publications of such a high standard.'

# COMMUNITY LIFE

As we no longer have such a thing as 'society' (if we are to believe Margaret Thatcher), 'community' seems to have replaced it as a word to suggest a notion of our shared values. The very word itself brings to mind the idea of people sharing or holding ideas or interests in common, going beyond the vital but essentially selfish confines of the family and the individual. It is also a seemingly less remote word than 'society', suggesting a closer, more local relationship.

We have tried to reflect this sense of shared experience among local people in our choice of pictures in this section. There are, therefore, images of activities which united the community in some way or other. There are the annual events, such as the carnivals and feast days, where there is a public face to community activities. There are also the special occasions, such as coronations, royal jubilees or the ending of World War One, when everybody gets together to celebrate.

The Peak District has, of course, acquired its own distinctive customs and ceremonies over the centuries, so there are a number of pictures that reflect this. There are the well dressing festivals, celebrating the life-enhancing qualities of fresh water, which date back to pagan times. Although they did suffer comparative neglect in many places in the past, they have re-emerged as something worth cherishing, especially in our more heritage-conscious age.

We have also tried to show a quieter, less obvious manifestation of community life. Although we live in a secular age, we should not underestimate the role the churches have played in fixing our notions of what community means. There are images that represent their contribution, such as those of a choir in a parish church and the celebration of the harvest in a Methodist chapel.

**Buxton, well dressing festival in the Crescent, 1864**
This print shows the festival attended by the fashionable visitors and citizens of Buxton. Advertisements talk of the fountains and the town in general being decorated with flowers and of other attractions such as brass bands, old English sports, fireworks and morris dancing by young girls. In spite of the idyllic, festive atmosphere depicted in the print, the reality may have been slightly different. The *Derby Reporter* speaks of cold, drenching rain, which made 'the triumphal arches look sadly disconsolate', and that the amusements were not worthy of Buxton, 'some shows of very small fry, jimcracks, shooting galleries, etc'.

**Buxton, well dressing at the Market Place, *c.*1900**
Water has made the most important contribution to the history and development of Buxton. It was the health-giving quality of the water from its springs that had built its reputation as a spa town since mediaeval times. It is, therefore, highly appropriate that the town should be one of the communities that had a well dressing festival to celebrate its water sources. The inscription reads 'And the woman said unto him, Sir, give me this water, that I thirst not, neither come hither to draw' from the Gospel of St John, chapter 4 verse 15.

**Tissington, well dressing, *c.*1900**
The well dressing at Tissington is one of the best known, taking place every Ascension Day. It is said to be the oldest well dressing in the county, dating back to the period of the Black Death in 1348–49 when the low number of deaths there was attributed to the purity of the water. In spite of occasions when there have been severe droughts, the wells have always been able to supply water to the inhabitants of the village. This particular well, one of five, is the Hall Well, close to the ancestral home of the FitzHerbert family, Tissington Hall.

Published courtesy of the *Derby Evening Telegraph*, DCHQ0005511

**Tissington, making of well dressing, 1981**

Making a well dressing is a time-consuming job. A framework, made of wooden boards, is covered with clay, which has been mixed with water and salt to an even consistency. The clay surface is made level, a previously-prepared drawing is put on top of it, and the design is then pricked into it. The outlines of the drawing are made to stand out with small cones, berries or beans, and then the picture is filled in, first with longer lasting materials such as pieces of bark, mosses and lichen, and then petals of flowers are added, being gently pressed into the clay.

Published courtesy of the *Derby Evening Telegraph*, DCHQ0006504

**Bakewell, well dressing, 1982**

The ancient tradition of well dressing is one that is almost unique to Derbyshire and the Peak District. Believed to derive ultimately from the ritual worship of springs and wells in pagan times, it involves decorating water sources with pictures made from petals and other plant material. Different local community groups devote a tableau to a particular subject or scene, and this one was created by the 2nd Bakewell Brownie-Guides. Most of the festivals are modern revivals of old traditions, and this is the case with Bakewell, where well dressing was revived in 1971.

**Ashford in the Water, garlands in the church, 1933**

These five garlands are a striking reminder of the ancient custom of making garlands to commemorate young women who died unmarried. The garlands were made of white paper in the form of rosettes, flowers and ribbons, attached to bell-shaped wooden frames, with paper gloves or handkerchiefs inside. The garland was carried on the girl's coffin to the funeral and then hung up in the church for posterity. What is remarkable is that the earliest one was in memory of Anne Howard, who had died as long ago as 1747, and that four of the five here still exist.

**Castleton, Garlanding procession, c.1960**

One of the ceremonies unique to the Peak District is the Garlanding at Castleton. It is held on 29 May, Oak Apple Day, commemorating the Restoration of King Charles II. A 'king' and a 'queen' are led on horseback in a procession through the town, the 'king' being crowned, so to speak, with the enormous garland, which covers half his body. Although there is a real historical background to the ceremony, the garland seems to hark back to earlier celebrations of the month of May, bringing to mind the pagan figure of the Green Man.

Published courtesy of the *Derbyshire Times*, DCHQ006575.

**Castleton, preparing for the Garland Ceremony, 1979**

This photograph shows the garland being carefully lowered over the 'king', who is in clothing of the Stuart period. It consists of a bell-shaped frame covered with leaves and wild flowers, and on the top of it is placed a bunch of flowers known as the Queen Posy. Its unusual shape derives from the church bell-ringers who originally made it. The weight of the garland is taken by leather straps over the shoulder, but it must be distinctly uncomfortable to wear, particularly as the procession frequently stops at various places for dancing by children before reaching its final destination at the church.

DCHQ006526

**Taddington, Club Feast Day, c.1922**

The members of the 'Adventurers of the Peak' Lodge proudly show off their banner. The lodges of the Independent Order of Oddfellows in Taddington held their Club Feast Day every year on Whit Sunday. It was an occasion when the whole village and many others from neighbouring communities took the opportunity to share in the experience. In the morning there would be a procession to the parish church, where a thanksgiving service was held. After it, another procession would take place and then the members would take themselves off to the club feast itself at the George Hotel.

## Taddington, maypole dancers, 1913

This is an image from the days when the term pole-dancing had a much more innocent flavour. Although it is generally assumed that only young girls took part in the traditional dances, we can clearly see that boys were included on this occasion. The schoolmistress, Mrs Beaven, is the lady standing on the left, who would have made sure the dancers were properly rehearsed. It is taking place on the afternoon of the Oddfellows Club Feast Day (13 May), and one of the lodge banners can be seen behind the maypole, which has been set up in front of the George Hotel.

## Taddington, Morris Dancers, *c.*1900

On the evening of the Oddfellows Club Feast Day, more processions took place in which morris dancing played a central part. In this unique photograph we can see that the procession has temporarily come to a halt, and the dancers are performing to the music being supplied by a brass band, which can made out on the right in front of a banner. Members in their sashes are crossing between each other, with their white handkerchiefs down by their knees rather than raised high in the air. Working their way down the village, they wisely stopped at every pub to revive their energy levels.

**Tideswell, morris dancing, _c._1950**

Tideswell has a long tradition for morris dancing, which goes back over 200 years, the earliest reference to it being recorded in 1797. Dancing used to take place during the Whitsuntide and Wakes weeks, on local feast days and at times of national celebrations. The dancers here are just in mid-air, having jumped up in time to the music provided by two accordionists. They are dressed in the garb we normally associate with it, including hats with flowers and ribbons, handkerchiefs in pockets and pads of little bells on shins. There is also a Fool, a burlesque character in stripy trousers.

**Bakewell Carnival, _c._1925**

Bakewell has long had a thriving carnival, which has continued to get many local organisations and societies involved, normally attracting large crowds to the town in most years. This particular float takes the form of a boat christened _Kathanode_, which is a brand name for one of the type of batteries made by the Dujardin-Planté Company, probably better known as the DP Battery Company, who were a large employer in the town until 1966. A lorry has literally become part of the boat, and you can see the wheels underneath the 'waves' and that the driver's cab has become the 'bridge'.

**Buxton Carnival Rose Queen, c.1925**

The carnival is an annual event in Buxton and coincides with the well dressings. As is usual with such events, a local girl is chosen as a queen to preside over the festivities, with the title of Rose Queen, which is appropriate given the flowery theme of well dressings. Here she is shown with her several attendants, including two young girls, somewhat improbably with fanfare trumpets, in front of the Mayor, local officials and several ladies with children in tow. They are on the steps of the local Cenotaph, which was set up by public subscription on the Slopes in 1920.

Buxton Museum, DCBM100498

H. Hinge. DMAG00341

**Ashbourne, Hospital Day celebrations, c.1920**

The horse and chaise carriage has stopped at Ashbourne Station during the Hospital Day celebrations. People have dressed up in fancy dress to take part in the event, which was being held to raise funds on behalf of one of the hospitals, which no doubt would have appreciated any boost to its coffers. On the back of the chaise stand two trumpeters, fanfaring the departure of the cortège before it sets off on its way around Ashbourne. At the side a 'joker' leans nonchalantly on the chaise wheel, apparently already in character.

### Matlock, volunteers for World War One, 1914

These three young men are believed to be the first volunteers in Matlock who enlisted in the armed forces at the outset of World War One in August 1914. It was a scene replicated throughout the country, as recruiting fever burst into life, urging many young men to rush into becoming involved in the 'war to end all wars'. They are standing in front of the railway station before setting off on their journey. The men were described in the local newspaper as 'Matlock Patriots', their names being G. Crowder, H. Holmes and Stanley Cocking.

### Buxton, soldiers at the Railway Station, *c.*1918

There is no doubt that this image dates from World War One, as soldiers march their way out of the Railway Station. At the very start of the war, Buxton was selected as a suitable place for training the newly-raised battalions of the Sherwood Foresters, the local regiment. By the end of the war the size of the regiment had swelled from eight battalions to 33, many of which would have been through Buxton at some stage. This time a number of people shelter under umbrellas, braving the weather to welcome the troops as they head off towards their billets.

### Buxton, Peace Day Parade, 1919

Celebrations took place on 19 July 1919 throughout the whole country to mark the end of World War One, as confirmed by the signing of the Treaty of Versailles the month before. This was the parade of the National Federation of Discharged and Demobilised Sailors and Soldiers. The spectacular procession had started at Fairfield Common, moving through the town, including the Slopes and Terrace Road, until it reached the Crescent, where speeches were made by civic dignitaries. 'It was a most impressive and moving occasion as the people believed they had emerged triumphantly from "a war that was to end war".'

### Bradbourne, Jubilee event, 1887

This photograph shows the extravagant display set up by the parishioners to celebrate the Golden Jubilee of Queen Victoria on 20 June 1887. This was the first real occasion when the ruling monarch was fêted in this way, and it marked a real shift in her popularity and that of the royal family in general. On the display Victoria is described as 'Queen of many nations', with the names of Albert George and Alexandra to the sides. They were her son and his wife, later to be King Edward VII and his Queen Consort.

**Bradbourne, Diamond Jubilee bonfire, 1897**

Bradbourne was to celebrate another Jubilee, this time for Queen Victoria's 60th anniversary as sovereign. On the day (Tuesday 22 June) there was a whole raft of events, including a service at the church, the laying of a foundation stone for a memorial lamp, teas and sport events for children and adults, and a concert and dance. The evening would have been rounded off by the lighting of the bonfire at the official time of 10 o'clock. It was one of a whole network of beacons throughout the country, which numbered no less than 2,500.

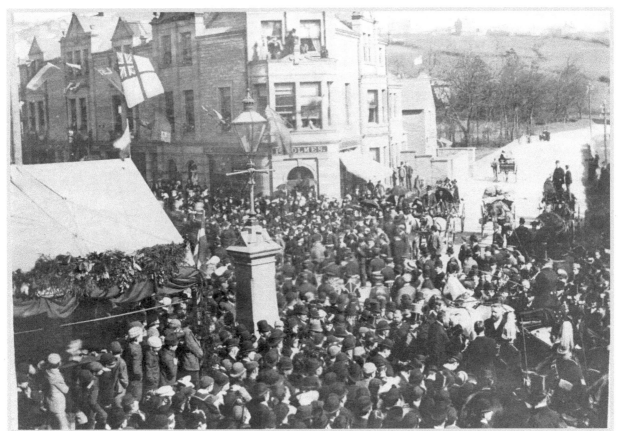

**Matlock, Queen Victoria's Diamond Jubilee, 1897**

The crowds congregated on Crown Square to take part in the celebrations for the Diamond Jubilee, which took place on 22 June 1897. Matlock Urban District Council had voted £100 to be spent on the festivities, including all the bunting and decorations. Fortunately the weather was good and the celebrations passed off successfully, as they did up and down the whole country. There were thanksgiving services, dinners and treats for young and old people alike, community singing, music and sporting events, all rounded off by a bonfire and fireworks in time-honoured fashion.

**Matlock, Coronation Day, 1911**

The good citizens of Matlock are dressed up in their best finery to celebrate the Coronation of King George V and Queen Mary on 22 June 1911. The ladies in particular have taken the opportunity to wear their large broad-rimmed hats to go with their summer blouses and skirts. The 'Welcome to Ye Old Town' sign straddling Church Street refers to that part of Matlock where the oldest buildings survive, which is the area around St Giles parish church, well away from the later developments at Matlock Bank and Matlock Bridge.

**Hathersage, Jubilee procession, 1935**

In May 1935 the Silver Jubilee of the reign of King George V was celebrated all over the country. Here we can see the Jubilee procession making its way through the village of Hathersage. Nancy Ibbotson had just been crowned as the Jubilee May Queen and she was accompanied by her retinue of Maids of Honour, who were Mary Arnfield, Returah Thompson, Muriel Ollerenshaw, Phyllis Armfield, Katherine Peet, Peggy Wilson, Joan Andrew and Sadie Wilson. Behind them were decorated drays, a fashion parade, schoolchildren and representatives of other village organisations.

### Bonsall, villagers at the Cross, c.1910

This image shows a sizeable proportion of the villagers of Bonsall on the 13 steps of the Market Cross. It seems to have been the practice to get as many people on the monument as possible whenever there was a community celebration of some sort, such as for a coronation or May Day. The market cross is the proud symbol of Bonsall and its close-knit community, most of whose livelihood used to be centred on lead mining and agriculture until recent times. Bonsall was never actually a market town, but the cross is now thought to have been there for over 600 years.

### Bonsall, adoption of Charles White as Liberal candidate, 1910

Bonsall Cross is again the focal point of celebration. This time we know the cause for it. Charles White was a cobbler who lived in Bonsall and became greatly involved in politics for the Liberal Party in West Derbyshire. He was adopted as a candidate for them in the general election of 1910 but lost his contest to Lord Kerry, in what is generally a safe Conservative constituency. He gained his reward, however, when he was elected as an MP in 1918, having built up a reputation as the people's champion. He can be seen here on the right, second row back.

*[NB a photograph of Lord Kerry's horse and trap is pictured in Transport and Travel]*

**Eyam, Plague Service, c.1909**

This photograph shows the large crowd that has assembled for the annual Plague Commemorative Service. Eyam was the village that famously quarantined itself off during an outbreak of plague, the inhabitants having made their own selfless decision to help stop the spread of the disease. It is believed 260 died as a result, more than half the population. During the outbreak the church was closed, but services were still held in the open air at Cucklett Delf near the village. On the last Sunday of August a service is held at that site to commemorate the heroic sacrifice made by the villagers.

**Bradwell, church bells, 1938**

The bells are lined up outside the church, ready to be put up in the tower. There were eight brand new bells, a generous gift from a Mrs Fanny Jeffery, who also paid for chimes to the church clock, an electric ringing apparatus and the costs of strengthening the tower to accommodate it all. They were a memorial for Samuel Fox, her mother's brother, who had himself been a generous benefactor to the church. The people assembled are: (left to right) Mr Ashton, Mr Walmsley, Harvey Hallam, Chetham Fletcher and Reverend Henry Edwin St John Southwell-Keely, the Vicar of Bradwell, 1936–44.

**Ashbourne, carol service, 1957**
The annual carol service at Ashbourne is taking place in front of the Christmas tree set up on the Market Place. At that time the event seemed to symbolise the close community spirit that existed in the town. The Methodist School Choir is joined by the townspeople behind them, as they sing out the familiar tunes. This event still continues to take place towards the end of December, usually on the last Sunday before Christmas.

**Peak Forest, church choir, 1964**
The choir can be seen practising for a dedication service following restoration work in the parish church. It is one of a number of churches that were dedicated to King Charles I. Although he was undoubtedly one of the worst monarchs ever to rule the country, he did manage to end up being regarded as something of a martyr for the Church of England following his execution in 1649. It was a 'peculiar' church, being outside the normal jurisdiction of a bishop and diocesan authorities, and it became notorious as a place where eloping couples could marry, a Gretna Green of the Midlands.

Published courtesy of the *Buxton Advertiser*, DCEP00437

Buxton Museum, DCBM1006578

### Chelmorton Primitive Methodist Church, *c.*1909

The Methodist Church was an important organisation in many local communities, providing an alternative form of Christian worship to the Anglican church and contributing much to the social fabric. Chelmorton seems to have been one of the earliest places where Methodism took hold, dating back as far as 1756 for its first congregation. Its fortunes fluctuated over the years, but by the time this photograph was taken it had regained a healthily-sized congregation. The circuit minister for Buxton, Henry Lowe Herod, sits in the middle, while the only other identifiable person is Walter Prime, son of Henry, second from the right on the back row.

DCHQ006500

### Darley Dale, Methodist Church Harvest Festival, 1921

The harvest festival has always been a special occasion for the community, a time to celebrate and be thankful for the successful outcome of the harvest. This time it has obviously yielded a bumper crop, as the pulpit area groans under the weight of produce brought in by church members at Dale Road Wesleyan Methodist Church. The notice above it all aptly quotes from the Bible, Galatians chapter 6, verse 7, 'Whatsoever a man soweth, that shall he also reap.' The church itself was built in 1904, and is still used as a place of worship.

**Two Dales, Wesleyan Methodist Sunday School parade, *c*.1910**

Everybody is dressed in their Sunday best for the parade in Two Dales, a hamlet in Darley Dale, including two boys ready with their drums. Sunday school was an important institution that helped to establish the presence of many religious denominations within the local community. Primarily focusing on study of the Bible, and normally linked to a church service, they were largely informal teaching sessions led by lay men and women. As the banner proclaims, the one at Two Dales was established in 1860, the Wesleyan Methodists having had a presence in the hamlet since at least 1827.

**Farley, Congregational Church Sunday School treat, *c*.1914**

This shows four horse-drawn carriages as they are about to set off on their way, loaded with what must have been almost the total population of Farley, a hamlet on the hillside north of Matlock. The Congregational Church at Farley Hill was opened in 1902, with the sad irony that its very first service was for the funeral of its founder, the Revd Edwin Clarke, who had died suddenly not long before it was due to open. The horses and carriages belonged to the Allen family, who also provided all the drivers.

**Darley Dale, memorial at Whitworth Institute, 1894**

Sir Joseph Whitworth (1803–1887) was the outstanding engineer of his generation and also a noted philanthropist. The community of Darley Dale, where he made his home, particularly benefited from his generosity, and funds from his will provided the means to build an institute with many facilities for the use of inhabitants. A memorial in memory of Sir Joseph was set up in 1894, and we can see the unveiling ceremony as it takes place. Note the man in the straw boater sitting on the steps to the left, who is probably a reporter taking notes on what is being said.

**Darley Dale, Charles Dawson's funeral, 1928**

This impressively regular procession is working its way down Church Road towards St Helen's Church. The front of the cortège, including men carrying wreaths, has gone past the Church Inn and is just about to reach the level crossing, while the end of the procession has not yet made it into Church Road. There are other photographs that show that it was even longer, with other walkers and a brass band on the march. The funeral was for Charlie Dawson, manager of Stancliffe Quarries, whose workforce would have made up most of the men walking along.

**Matlock, Civil Defence training course, 1962**

A team of vicars learn more about Geiger counters, devices to detect levels of radioactivity. The blackboard behind them gives an indication as to why members of the clergy were receiving such training. In the event of a nuclear catastrophe they, as respected pillars of the community, were needed to provide help and guidance to survivors, in terms of both their physical and spiritual welfare. It may all seem slightly unreal now, but this course took place in the months just before the Cuban Missile Crisis, when the world really did seem to be tottering on the brink of nuclear war.

**Buxton Fire Brigade outside the Town Hall, *c.*1890**

This fine body of men represents the Town Fire Brigade. Smartly attired in their uniform and navy-style caps, they have been seated to have their group photograph taken outside the Town Hall when there is still snow on the ground, which should make it winter, although you can never be sure in Buxton. The fire brigade had been maintained by the Devonshire Estate until the setting-up of the elected Local Board in 1859. This photograph must have been taken some time after 1889, as this was when the Town Hall was completed, a symbol of civic pride.

**Matlock Police Force, 1924**

This picture was taken outside the Town Hall on Bank Road, opposite the old Police Station. It shows the police force for the Matlock Division of the Derbyshire Constabulary, taken on 15 November 1924. All the individuals are named as follows: (back row, left to right) PCs Barker, Stanton, Jess, McDonald, Neild, Lester, Phipps, Bateson and Simpson; (front row) PC Davies, Sergeant Ridd, Superintendent Aves, Mr Tom Wright JP, the Chairman of the Police Committee, Mr J.S. Potter, Clerk to the Magistrates, Inspector Kennedy, Sergeant Cappendell and PC Bulpitt.

**Great Hucklow, theatre production, 1930**

The community theatre group, the Great Hucklow Village Players, was set up by the author and broadcaster Lawrence du Garde Peach in 1927. The actors and the stage crew were made up of local people, and although they were an amateur organisation they prided themselves on the professionalism of the productions they put on. Peach was the main driving force, providing many scripts, the most interesting of which were the Derbyshire Comedies, plays in local dialect. This particular photograph is from a production of *The Rivals* by Sheridan. The actors shown are Marianne Peach, Margaret Dickie, Joe Hancock and Mr Peach himself.

**Matlock, the Thorntree Inn, c.1920**

The pub has been, and hopefully always will be, an important part of community life. The Thorntree is the perfect example of a small, unpretentious pub with friendly locals. The people here look happy and relaxed in spite of the fact that they don't seem to be in possession of any beer yet. They have taken the trouble to look reasonably smart, making them a good deal more presentable than the average pub-goer these days. The sign above the door proclaims George W. Marsden as the landlord of the pub, and we know from trade directories that he was there from at least 1916 to 1932.

# GROWING UP

These are a collection of images taken in the Peak District which show children growing up. We have tried to include pictures of different aspects of childhood, encompassing the whole age range from tot to teenager.

Attending school is obviously an important part of any child's life, and there are several images to reflect this. The formal class photographs here have been chosen in the hope that they show a little more about the children than most of these pictures generally do. In some photographs, for example, in the period before designated school uniforms were introduced, there are particular differences in the way the pupils have been dressed, which may perhaps indicate the expectations, or lack of them, of their parents.

In general, the way children used to dress, or be dressed, is an important part of the appeal of these particular pictures. Some show the somewhat romanticised images that parents used to construct for their own children, in the form of sailor suits and Little Lord Fauntleroy outfits. Others show teenagers dressed as little adults, in that unimaginable time before there was even any concept that they were somehow different from their parents.

There are also pictures showing children having fun in various ways, play being of course a much more congenial way of spending time than anything done at school. There are also pictures of children dressing up, taking part in theatrical productions and making their own entertainment.

Most of the images show the innocent, positive side of childhood, but there are also a number which highlight the crueller, more negative aspects of life in the past. Pictures taken at St Andrew's orphanage home are a reminder to us that not all children had an easy start in life. The sight of young people among the staff of Smedley's Hydro hints at the economic reality that underpinned life until only very recently, namely that most children had to grow up pretty quickly and earn a living for themselves or for other members of their family.

**Ashbourne, infant child of H. Hansen, c.1906**
This little girl has been identified as Alice Emma Hansen, daughter of the photographer Hans Peter Hansen and his wife Mary-Jane. She was the youngest of five children born to the couple. They had suffered the trauma of the early death of one of their other children, Doris Emma, in 1900 when the baby was only a few months old. Perhaps that loss may have prompted the couple to take such a relaxed and intimate photograph of their infant playing on a rug.

**Matlock, young girl at Smedley's Hydro, *c.*1900**
This photograph was taken among the plants in the Winter Gardens in the grounds of Smedley's Hydro. The photographer was Alfred Seaman, who seems to have frequently undertaken work on behalf of the hydro. Although the child has been identified as a girl, it could just possibly have been a boy. It was the convention of the time to put boys in dresses until they 'breeched', or started wearing trousers, which took place between the ages of three and eight. To the relief of most boys, no doubt, this particular practice was abandoned around the time of World War One.

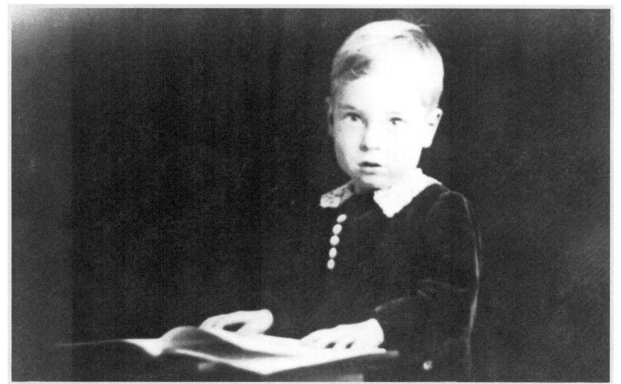

**Matlock, boy with book, *c.*1925**
This young boy of Holly Bank in Matlock has been shown in a somewhat idealised light. If not quite having the full Little Lord Fauntleroy look, with his hair cut short, he is still wearing a velvet suit and lace collar, an image of the 'good little boy' which mothers continued to hanker for in spite of all evidence to the contrary. The boy is also shown with a book, suggesting a precocious intellectual talent. This was another convention of the time, usually well divorced from any reality as far as such young boys were concerned.

**Buxton, boy in toy car, 1933**

Young Ben Ash is driving his toy car in the garden of his home at London Road in Buxton. He must have been a really good boy to have earned the right to be given it by his parents, Joseph and Caroline. A toy like this would have been something really special then. The bodies were made of solid sheet metal, and it looks like there were plenty of ornamental features, such as a windscreen, mudguards and lights. Pedal-powered cars were sometimes given away by companies that made real cars as an extra little perk for fathers when they bought one.

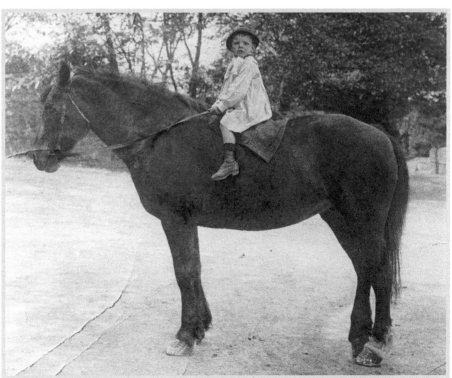

**Wensley, boy on horse, c.1900**
The name of the small boy in his smock and felt hat on the big horse is Joe Clay. There were several farmers called Clay at that time, and he is likely to have been a son of one of them. He shows absolutely no fear of falling off, managing to sit up straight, hold the reins and look towards the photographer all at the same time. The horse was most likely a working animal on a farm and, therefore, docile enough for someone to have put a child on its back.

**Bamford, children at play, c.1900**

Here we can see children gathered at the Green in Bamford, a small triangular plot of land. A boy practises his putting technique, while the rest of the children stand or lounge around. Some of them have clambered over a pile of stones gathered together as part of the monument to commemorate Queen Victoria's Diamond Jubilee. Young children were warned not to play in the water-filled stone troughs there, presumably for fear of drowning, but as with most such warnings they just did it anyway and took their punishment when they went home with socks and shoes wet through.

**Winster, pancake race, 1981**

The pancake races at Winster have been an annual tradition for over a hundred years now. They take place on Shrove Tuesday, which is the last day in the calendar before Lent, when all the eggs, milk and flour have to be used up before fasting. On this particular day, which was a very chilly one when coats definitely needed to stay on, there were several races for boys, girls and adults. The boys' races were won by Leon Jackson, Andrew Gilbert and Phillip Davidson. One unfortunate boy, however, when tossing his pancake, managed to lose it down a drain.

**Cromford, girl looking at birds in a cage, 1864**
The girl in the photograph is named as Helen Arkwright. She appears in a photograph album maintained by the Arkwright family of Willersley. It is thought that she is Mary Helen, born in 1857, the daughter of Arthur W. Arkwright of Broughton Astley, Leicestershire, and great-granddaughter of the pioneering industrialist Sir Richard Arkwright. The owning of birds as pets was popular among the wealthier families of the Victorian age, but the pose of the girl might suggest some ambivalence as she looks at them in a cage.

**Darley Bridge, lady and boy at gate, 1907**
A lady and a boy, presumably her son, have gone for a walk in the area around Darley Bridge. The smartly-dressed lady has stopped by a gate for a photograph, but the boy in his school cap has turned away, not bothering to take part. Is he having a bit of a sulk? Perhaps he is put out at being dragged out for a walk by his mother. Looking at it the other way, perhaps he would have liked to carry on, but she has decided to go no further. Or did he just not realise the photograph was being taken?

**Buxton, first communion at St Anne's Church, 1948–49**

Aged about seven or eight, these Buxton children look happy on the occasion of their first communion. An important day in the life of any child brought up as a Catholic, it has a resonance that lasts well into adulthood. Traditionally this used to take place on a Saturday in May, and girls would wear a special new white outfit. St Anne's Roman Catholic Church was opened on Terrace Road in July 1861, financed by Samuel Grimshawe of Errwood Hall, and is still involved with young people today, having links with St Thomas More Catholic School and St Anne's Primary School.

Buxton Museum, DCBM000210

Mr F. Winfield, DCHQ006612

**Matlock, the Cliffe 'Back Yard Team', c.1920**

These young men proudly take up the poses adopted for football team photographs since time immemorial. Staring straight and purposefully into the camera, with folded arms, they all look as if they mean business. Even if they are only going to be having a kick-about in a backyard they do have a proper ball, so it was something to take seriously. No doubt there were plenty of cuts and bruises after the end of the game. It is likely that these are boys from the St Andrew's Boys Home, which was formerly known as the Cliffe.

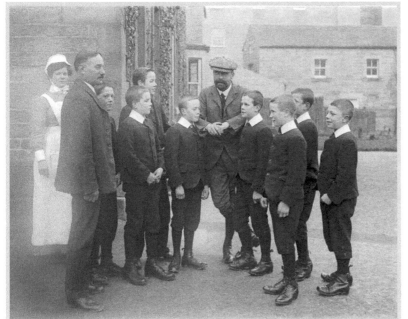

**Matlock, boys from St Andrew's Home, c.1904**

The businessman and local benefactor Ernest Bailey established a boys' residential home in 1901. It was in his old house, close to one of the mills in Lower Lumsdale, where he gained his wealth. The home was renamed after the saint on whose feast day (30 November) it happened to be opened. It was established under the auspices of the Church of England Society for Providing Homes for Waifs and Strays, and provided accommodation for 34 boys, who were orphans or the products of broken homes. This is almost certainly Mr Bailey (in the cap) with some of his charges.

**Matlock, dinner at St Andrew's Home, c.1904**

All the boys are sitting down for a meal outside. There was a dining room inside, but it was a bit too cramped for a good photograph. The age range was usually between eight and 14, and we can see how they have been grouped together by age. The boys received their education at schools in Tansley and Matlock, although some of the older ones went to the local grammar school, also founded by Ernest Bailey. For many, his influence would continue to be felt in their adult lives, as they went on to find work in his mills.

### Matlock, choir from St Andrew's Home, c.1904

Boys from the home regularly made up the choir that served St John's Chapel, a small but picturesque Anglican chapel hidden away among the trees covering the hillsides between Matlock and Matlock Bath. The home would frequently resound with music, as the boys practised their parts for church services. Occasionally they would also sing at All Saints Church on Matlock Bank, which was often used by visitors staying at Smedley's and the other hydros. Although it was no doubt a chore for some of the boys, the choir did provide a point of contact with the wider local community.

### Buxton, Mrs Kettle's Private School, c.1880

These nine girls were under the guidance of Mrs Elizabeth Radford Kettle (c.1809–1888), originally from Cromford. She ran what was known as a Dame School, a type of establishment which has generally acquired a poor reputation. Mrs Kettle would not have had any teaching qualifications as such, but she would have drawn on her previous experience as a governess to help educate her charges. If they were lucky the girls might have received training in the 'feminine accomplishments' of French, music, drawing and needlework. If not, they may have got little more than the basic skills in reading and writing.

J.S. Billingham, DCHQ006584

**Darley Dale, Churchtown School group, 1900**

This is a fine photograph of a group of scholars at the Churchtown Church of England School. The stern-looking man with the impressive moustache on the right is almost certainly Charles S. Anthony, the schoolmaster, while the young lady right at the back could be his wife, Julia. They are all smartly dressed up for the occasion, with some boys wearing the belts of their Church Lads Brigade uniform (one even has his cap). The very young boy wearing the Little Lord Fauntleroy outfit is probably Cyril, the son of Charles and Julia, hopefully immune from any potential ridicule.

DCHQ04576

**Taddington, White's School, 1908**

White's School was a charity school founded in 1804 under the terms of the will of Michael White, who left provision for the free education of poor children in the village. This type of institution was often the only chance many children had of receiving any form of education until the late 19th century. Here the headteacher Miss Catherine Beaven is on the right. Her assistant Miss Helen G. Moss (on the left), who was the daughter of a local innkeeper, aged about 16, would herself have been a pupil at the school.

**Hassop RC School group, *c.*1917**
It was unusual for the only school of a small village like Hassop to be a Roman Catholic one. It was erected in 1859 and attached to the church built by the Eyre family, who were prominent Catholics. Here we can see the young teacher Miss Emily Dykes with her class outside. Among the children are Phillip Kennedy (front row, second boy on left) and his sister (second row, first left). Other children include Billy Bromley (front row, third boy from left) and three Widdowson sisters named Cissie, Alice and Bella. Unfortunately, the school was eventually closed in 1930.

**Dove Holes C of E School group, 1923**
The Dove Holes Church of England School was founded in 1883 to cater for the children of the village that had sprung up to house the families of the men who were working in the several quarries opened during the 19th century. The teacher pictured on the left is Miss Froggatt. The names of the pupils are Donald Kaye, Geoffrey Kaye, Arthur Marchington, Ivan Hall, Bill Holmes, Renee Sidebotham, Beatrice Fox, Florence Garner, Dick Booth, Emily Needham, Herbert Bradwell, Charlie Greenhalgh, Winster Stone, Marian Alsop, Edith Garner and Eunice Cross.

**Matlock Council School group, 1928**
This photograph shows pupils wearing a surprisingly different array of their best school clothes. Several wear the old-style Eton collars, a couple with bow ties as well. One boy at the front has a sailor suit on, while the young man standing on the extreme right has a wing collar and even seems to be sporting a flower in his button-hole. Three have blazers, while the rest sport jackets and ties. Only one seems to have come in an ordinary jumper. The headmaster, J. Mills, is on the left, overseeing the group.

**Middleton, teacher with small class, *c.*1955**
Middleton and Smerrill School was one of the hundreds of village schools that used to be a mainstay of rural community life. Here, Mary B. Thompson teaches a group of children who actually comprise the whole school. They must have benefited from the individual attention small class numbers could provide, something which is confirmed by an inspector's report of the time, who complimented the skills of the experienced headmistress. Unfortunately, as with many such schools of this size, it became unsustainable in the eyes of the educational authorities to keep it going, and the school was closed in 1972.

**Bamford, empty school classroom, c.1950**

This is the inside of an empty classroom at Bamford Primary School in the middle of the last century. There are desks with ink wells, into which pupils would dip old-fashioned nib pens, and real blackboards on which are written in chalk some basic, if now largely redundant, information on pounds, shillings and pence, and imperial weights and measures. There are maps of the world on the wall and even a speaker to take school radio from the BBC. It looks as if it might be a bit cramped, but this would still be a problem 50 years later.

**Bakewell, netball at Lady Manners School, 1909**

Although the information supplied with this picture was that it featured a match between the junior teachers and fifth form pupils (the latter winning comfortably by 14 goals to one), it seems more like a netball shooting contest rather than an actual game, probably on the occasion of the annual sports day. It is taking place in front of quite a few interested male spectators, some of whom have encroached on the pitch. Netball had been introduced to the school in the previous year at the suggestion of the headmaster's wife, Mrs Jemmett, to provide some physical recreation for the girls.

**Buxton, Cavendish Girls School Sports Day, c.1920**

Unless you were of a sporting disposition, one of the traumas of school life used to be the ritual of the annual sports day. Here, girls in their gymslips and woollen tights are coming to the end of a race round the boundary of the playing field, where a good-size crowd is watching from the banking. The winner has just reached the finishing line, but she seems to have slowed down already and could almost be walking. It as if she's saying to herself she's not going to take one step more than she has to.

**Darley Dale County School football team, 1948–49**

This is a fine group photograph of enthusiastic young boys ready to enjoy their football. The goalkeeper David Slack (standing in the middle) must have been a very athletic shot-stopper to make up for his smallness of stature, dwarfed as he is by the two giants standing next to him (G. Walker and B. Horobin). The teachers at the back are Mr Robinson, Mr Hancock, Mr Fearn and Mr Lomas. The rest of the boys are: (back row) Turner, Derek Marsden, G. Hickman, Ivor Smith; (front row) Bob Rouse, Maurice Watts, Cyril Walker, Roy Askew and Peter Ashworth.

**Children sledging, c.1950**

One of the advantages of living in an area like Buxton was the chance to take a sledge out after the snows came and have some fun. Pat on the left certainly seems to be enjoying herself judging by her smile. Eric on the right seems a little less sure about it, but he might only have been a bit shy or put out at having to stop and pose for the camera. The photograph was taken on Hall Bank by Frederick Walker, proprietor of the Savoy Hotel..

**Sledging at Temple Fields, 1969**

This shows what would seem to be a whole platoon of boys sledging their way down the slopes of Temple Fields. This became one of the most popular areas for people to get out on their sledges, once it was decided that it was all too much of a risky business to be done on the roads anymore. It still looks pretty risky on this occasion, and we can only guess at the number of casualties there must have been in the pile-up at the bottom.

DCHQ000226

Published courtesy of the Buxton Advertiser, DCHP000482

Buxton Museum, DCBM000023

**Sledging in Buxton, *c.*1947**
One disadvantage of going sledging is that you always have to make your way back to the top before you can do it again. There are certainly enough hilly slopes to choose from in the Peak District, and the children here seem to have chosen one of the steeper ones. There is a wall at the bottom with some snow in front to soften the impact, but there is not much of a slowing down area. When you are young, however, such considerations do not come into play.

DCHQ003607

**Matlock, Coronation Day party, 1911**
Coronations and other royal events always allowed children the chance to enjoy a day off school and have some fun. This party is taking place to celebrate the coronation of King George V on 22 June 1911. Everyone is, of course, all dressed up, as if he were personally going to turn up at any moment. It was the 'official party', being paid for out of the council rates. Residents further up Matlock Bank, however, felt somewhat neglected and decided to hold their own party, so some of these children may have had the chance to do it all over again.

**Matlock Bath, Sunday School party, 1962**

The children of Matlock Bath Sunday School are enjoying their Christmas party. It was held in the parochial hall of Holy Trinity Church, and was organised by the teachers. Forty children were given tea, played games and watched some films. As we can see, they also made their own entertainment along the way. Although the primary purpose of Sunday schools has always been to provide religious education, the bringing-together of children in a wide range of social activities also played its part in enforcing a sense of shared community values.

**Matlock, group of children in costume, c.1900**

The children of the Matlock Wesleyan Methodist Church have put on a variety of different costumes for a pageant, although the exact stories are not clear. One girl is wearing long biblical robes, another a crown on her head, several younger ones have all-white dresses on, and a boy cuts a dash in elaborate 18th-century clothing and a three-cornered hat. The group on the right is the most distinctive, with a pretend old lady, a cat, a dog, and a boy with a hood over his head.

**Ashbourne, amateur dramatics, c.1910**
Unfortunately, no details are available about the circumstances for this production of amateur dramatics. The large, high window suggests the interior of some sort of church or grand country house. Nine out of the troupe are definitely young females, and the tenth member is presumably one as well, sitting cross-legged on the floor with false whiskers and a crown in a decidedly unregal way. The girl standing above the rest is possibly playing an angel, or a fairy with a wand, in which case she might be modelled on Tinkerbell from the recent smash-hit *Peter Pan*, by J.M. Barrie.

**Matlock Bath, junior pantomime, 1959**

Here, youngsters are taking part in a performance of *Aladdin* by members of the Matlock Bath Holy Trinity Parish Church. They undertook their performance over three nights in December 1959, the proceeds of £12 3s going towards the worthy, if somewhat dull, cause of buying a new lamp for the church. No doubt the children were more excited by the cream cakes and jellies which their parents got together for them when the curtain came down on the final night, as a reward for the hard work they had put in over the previous few weeks.

**Dove Holes, carnival parade, 1957**

The idea of drum majorettes was imported into Britain from America after the end of World War Two. In the drab post-war decades it gave an opportunity for girls to dress up in colourful uniforms and express themselves with a collection of like-minded individuals. In the photograph album from which this image came, the troop are called 'The Dancers'. They are taking part in a parade during Dove Holes Carnival, blowing tuneless horns as they march along. The bystanders show admirable restraint in the face of such provocation.

**Matlock, Church Lads' Brigade, *c.*1910**

The various boys' brigade movements were set up to promote the ideals of discipline, self-respect and 'all that tends towards a true Christian Manliness' among boys. There was a strong military element to it, with heavy emphasis being put on drill, physical exercise, obedience of commands, and building team spirit. Boys regularly went to military-style camps, where the effectiveness of such training was reinforced. There were also uniforms and, as in this particular case, rifles. No doubt to the relief of other church members, these rifles were dummy ones, used purely for drill practice and parades.

**Bakewell, Church Lads' Brigade, *c.*1910**

The Church Lads' Brigade was an organisation set up by the Church of England in 1891 to attract boys into the Anglican community, people having taken note of the great success of the Nonconformist Boys' Brigade in reaching that particular target audience. The Bakewell branch has been photographed here at Bath Street. There was obviously a marching band element to them, as the drums sit on the ground and several boys in the front row hold pipes, flutes or bugles. At the back stand the older contingent, including two adult officers in their peak caps.

**Chatsworth, Tideswell Scout Group, 1965**

The Scouts were out in force at Chatsworth in June 1965. This was the occasion of the first Derbyshire International Scout Camp, cleverly known as the Ramboree. Four thousand camped out in the North Park, about half being Scouts from the home county. Here we can see the Scout group from Tideswell, who would have had the opportunity to meet other Scouts from all over the world. Overseas visitors found out the truth about English summers, as it rained constantly during the first few days and the site was on the verge of flooding before the weather relented.

**Matlock, Smedley's Hydro staff, *c.*1885**

As the raising of the school-leaving age to 18 continues to be an issue for political debate, it is sobering to think that, at the time this picture was taken, that particular limit stood at only 10 and there was even discretion in rural areas for children to leave earlier than that. For many girls of poorer families, employment prospects were limited mostly to domestic service. An institution like Smedley's Hydro would have used many girls to help with the laundry, cleaning, kitchen-work and other chores. Several girls appear in this photograph, as do a few boys.

Buxton Museum, DCBM/0535

**Buxton, Thomas and Agnes McKenzie, 1859**
This couple, presumably brother and sister, look quite at ease and relaxed in front of the camera. They are wearing clothes which were in fashion at that time. The girl is in a crinoline dress supported by a framework of hoops, although she would have been spared the inconvenience of wearing a bodice because of her age. The boy is wearing a pair of baggy trousers, with a very short waistcoat and a jacket buttoned very high up. They are actually the sort of clothes their parents would have worn as well, teenage rebellion not being part of life then.

**Bakewell, young lady, *c.*1860**

This young lady, Lois Theodosia Hodkin, was living at the Grange near Bakewell and aged about 15 at the time the photograph was taken. She is wearing a crinoline dress with a simple sloping-shoulder top, which was the popular style then, as was the straight-haired hairstyle. Born in Barlow near Chesterfield, Lois Theodosia was the daughter of a tailor and would later become a housemaid. In 1875 she would go on to marry William Herbert Dawson, a commercial traveller in the north-west, and the couple would have a family of at least four children.

# HOME AND FAMILY

Family photographs are often some of our most precious possessions. If people are asked to say what they would save from a house on fire, the family photographs are usually close to the top of any list. It is, therefore, something of a paradox that the people in many such photographs that end up in archives, libraries and similar repositories are not identified. Individuals generally know the identity of their own family members when they are taking their pictures and do not think to make a note for posterity of who, when and where. Unfortunately, the memory dims and this information is then lost in the passage of time.

A number of the photographs in this section suffer from the fact that the individuals are unidentified, but we can still derive something from them. For one thing we can see how people used to dress and how they used to look. After all, we still make judgements today on people we do not know by their appearance, and it is no different when we look at images of people from the past.

Photography in the early days was a laborious and expensive business, and posing in front of a camera was not usually a task undertaken lightly. People of the Victorian era can look very stiff and awkward to modern eyes, with rarely a smile to be seen, but this was caused mostly by the limitations of the technology, which required them to keep absolutely still for several seconds. Of course, they also wanted to project appropriate images of themselves which they hoped other people would see: the stern responsible father, the dutiful home-making wife, the respectful son, etc.

Some of the photographs here show families or owners outside their houses. They show the stone cottages typical of the Peak District with their occasionally rampant gardens. On the whole, there are few images actually taken inside proper homes. Again, technology meant that it was only the extraordinary interiors that people tended to think worth photographing.

**Ashbourne, Mrs Hansen and daughter, c.1907**

Here are the wife and youngest child of the Ashbourne photographer Hans Peter Hansen. He had married Mary-Jane Harden in 1892 when he had been a lodger at her widowed mother's home in Hull. Having moved to Ashbourne, a photographic studio was set up by them in Church Street. Mary-Jane would seem to have played her part in the family business when their children were older, but at this stage she would have been more involved in being a mother, particularly to the young girl in the chair by her feet, Alice Emma.

**Ashbourne, Hansen family children, c.1907**
This family scene shows three of the children of Hans Peter Hansen and his wife Mary-Jane. The girl is Elise Winifred (born 1898), the older boy George Henry (born 1895) and the younger boy Wilfred Thorvald (born 1902) with his racquet. Although it looks like a comfortable domestic scene at home, it has been shot in the photographic studio of their father. There was a plentiful supply of props to hand there, some of which appear in photographs made by him for other families.

**Matlock, family group, c.1910**
This is a picture taken in a professional photographer's studio believed to be in Matlock, showing a teenage girl and presumably her grandmother. The backcloth is not particularly realistic or well executed, but the classical style of architecture depicted might indicate the sitter's social aspirations, just as the books might suggest an inclination towards self-improvement through learning. The girl's dress is a fairly simple white one, made of a much lighter material than an adult's would have been. Her hair is held loosely rather than piled up, and care has been taken to ensure we can see how long it is.

52

**Matlock, woman writing, *c*.1910**

The image of the mother at her writing desk was something of a cliché used by photographers at the turn of the last century. She was usually shown writing in an account book, to suggest the idea that she was busy running the domestic household. In this case, the photographer has had to adapt that image a little, as his props do not seem to extend as far as a writing desk. The backdrop, chair and table are the same as for the teenage girl and her grandmother, so it is tempting to think that she might be the mother of this family.

Watford Museum, DCHQ005892

### Matlock, family group, *c.*1910

Although the mother is shown here with her two children, the setting is not particularly one of domestic bliss. We would have expected the shot of a home interior, whereas what we get is a simple canvas sheet for a backdrop. The photograph was actually taken outdoors as the ground beyond the rug and the drainpipe on the left clearly show. The family have obviously tried their best to be smart, so it is odd that the photographer seems to have taken less than the requisite care to get the best possible picture for them.

### Matlock, family in backyard, *c.*1910

This group photograph of a sister and her two younger brothers was taken by a Matlock professional photographer, who has undertaken his work at a client's home. He has managed to get a shot of the children looking away to his right rather than directly at the camera, presumably at the instigation of their parents. They have been told to be absolutely still while the photograph was taken, something which they have succeeded in doing admirably, particularly the older boy on the left who seems to be rigid with concentration.

Watford Museum, DCHQ005881

**Matlock, Else family, *c.*1890**
This is a photograph of the Else family at the front door of their home, the Firs, now Matlock branch library. This family was greatly involved in a famous legal dispute, known as the Great Matlock Will case. Following the death of the wealthy George Nuttall in 1856, John Else claimed to have found codicils to George's will which gave a large estate to him. After no less than three trials, in which alleged forgery of the codicils was the issue at stake, the verdict eventually went against Else in 1864. He was later to be an estate agent.

### Matlock Bath, Ellis family, c.1910

James Ellis and his wife Sarah (née Pratt) are outside their house, called Primrose Cottage, on St Johns Road in Matlock Bath. They are seated on the front row with their younger children James Junior, Annie and Frances. On the back row stand (from left to right) Ernest, who was killed in World War One, Winifred, Edith, Edwin, Gertrude and Alfred. James had worked for many years as a railway carter and would have been around 50 years of age when this photograph was taken. He was born in Blackfordby in Leicestershire and married Sarah Pratt in 1882.

### Matlock, Ballington family, c.1900

This is meant to be a group photograph of the Ballington family outside a house called Wellfield. It might seem unlikely that all these people are from the same family, but a look at the census returns of 1901 reveals a surprisingly high number of Ballingtons in Matlock, no fewer than 52 within the boundaries of the civil parish. Unfortunately, the exact occasion for this gathering is not known. They are all well turned out for it whatever it was, with a high proportion of smart-looking pieces of headgear, including several 'halo'-type hats for the very young.

## Matlock, Ballington family, 1913

This is the Ballington family outside their home at Wellfield on Matlock Bank. The parents are Edith Mary Elizabeth and Henry, who earned his living as a nurseryman. With them are their nine children. Standing beside father is Victor, while Thomas stands next to mother with the hand of his brother George resting on his shoulder. Behind them are Annie, Mary Deborah, Elizabeth, Harry and George, while at their feet sit the youngest Harold and Jessie, next to the family collie.

## Wensley, Walters family, c.1900

This is a group photograph of what is believed to be the family of William Walters of Wensley. He was the son of George Walters, a farmer at Cross Green, and was described as a park-keeper in the 1901 census returns, possibly working in the recreation grounds at the Whitworth Institute, set up after the death of the famous engineer, Sir Joseph Whitworth. His wife's name is believed to be Martha, who was originally from nearby Bonsall and had the maiden name of Bunting. She is holding their daughter, Dorothy, who is wearing one of the long gowns used for babies.

**Buxton, Prime family portrait,** *c.*1908

This is the family of Daniel and Agnes Prime. Daniel was born in Buxton about 1866, the youngest son of Henry Prime, who was a watchmaker. He and his wife Agnes were living at 9 Recreation Road, Buxton in 1901, when Daniel was working as a grocer's assistant. They look as if they might have prospered a little since then, as they are very smartly dressed, including sons Fred and Arnold in their sailor suits. The photograph is typical of its period, with a somewhat formal and unsmiling family group, but seems to hint at the personalities of its subjects.

**Cromford, Arkwright family group,** *c.*1865

This is a group photograph taken on the grass outside Willersley Castle. The patriarch, Peter Arkwright, sits with his wife, Mary Ann, in the midst of some of their offspring. The couple had married in 1805 and gone on to have no less than 17 children. This may well be the occasion of their 60th anniversary in September 1865. The only other named person here was Colonel Clowes (with the top hat), who was the father of a son who had married one of their daughters, Caroline Elizabeth.

### Fenny Bentley, Buckley family group, 1948

The photograph shows relatives of Canon Derek H. Buckley at a Christmas get-together. The home was probably that of a cousin in Fenny Bentley, as friends remember the family regularly gathering there for parties at Christmas. Canon Buckley himself was later Rector of Fenny Bentley with Thorpe and Tissington between 1959 and 1967. The photograph is framed in the doorway of the conservatory, and is comparatively relaxed and informal. Interestingly many members of the family would be wearing exactly the same clothes in a similar photograph the following year, suggesting something of the austerity which continued to prevail after wartime.

### Taddington, Annie Skidmore and Tommy, *c.*1910

Here is an old-fashioned perambulator or pram, in which Mrs Annie Skidmore has been pushing baby Tommy home. She is actually his great-aunt. They have stopped outside the house where they were living, known as Home Farm, and the old lady has sat the baby up, awash in all his white linen, so that they can be photographed. Prams were introduced during the reign of Queen Victoria, who apparently did much herself to raise their profile. Although the large wheels made them unwieldy at times, they were still highly desirable items.

Picture courtesy of Betty Wilkson via J. Wordingham. DCHQ004572

**Taddington, Home Farm,** *c.*1910

Annie Skidmore is this time standing by the wall, while the younger couple are attending to business by the door. It looks very much as if the man is being told, in no uncertain terms, that he is not going to be let into the house with those dirty boots on. He has been definitely identified as George Skidmore, and the younger woman is almost certainly his wife, Charlotte. Annie was actually George's aunt and she had been staying with her husband William at their home since at least 1901.

**Matlock, young couple, *c.*1914**
This is a picture of a young soldier and his recent bride who have made sure that her wedding ring is clearly visible. Although it was taken by a professional photographer, no care seems to have been taken to provide any sort of suitable backdrop. Plain backgrounds were common, but this one does not even attempt to hide the windows or cover all the wall. Perhaps the couple had made a snap decision to come in just before he left to fight and were just concerned with getting a picture of themselves, however it looked.

### Matlock, army couple, *c.*1914

This is an intriguing picture as the girlfriend, we presume, of the soldier dons a mate's uniform and stands to attention with a bayoneted rifle. In many ways this could be seen as an entirely appropriate image for World War One. It was the first time that civilians were mobilised, in effect, as part of the war effort. Women played a hugely significant role, taking up much of the work in factories, shops and offices and on the farms, most of which had previously been done by the vast numbers of men who were required for military service.

### Matlock, wedding group photograph, 1904

Emily Evans, only daughter of William Evans of Greenwich House, Dale Road, Matlock Bridge married Cecil Goward of Market Harborough on Tuesday 20 September 1904, at St Giles Parish Church, Matlock. The two bridesmaids, in ivory white silk trimmed with green, were the bridegroom's sister and niece, Miss Goward and Olive Duke. Also pictured among the guests are the bride's mother and father, and her brother Mr C.W. Evans, who was best man. The organist played the *Wedding March*, and the couple were showered with confetti. After a honeymoon in Scarborough the couple were to live in Market Harborough.

**Matlock, Bradbury family wedding photograph, 1925**
This photograph was taken after the wedding of Arthur Bradbury and Mary Deborah Ballington, outside the bride's family home at Wellfield. They were married at All Saints Church on Matlock Bank on 3 September 1925. On the right are the Ballington side of the family, with the bride's mother Edith sitting down, brother Harry behind her and her sister Jessie. The bride is wearing her best clothes rather than the custom-designed white dress, an item growing in popularity then but by no means universal. The bouquets she and the bridesmaids are carrying are truly sizeable, but this was customary for the period.

**Cromford, Arkwright family wedding, 1870**
On 19 April 1870 Edith Anne Arkwright married Richard Digby Cleasby, a barrister, at the church of St Mary's, Cromford, which was in effect the family church, having been built by Sir Richard Arkwright. Edith's parents, Edward and Charlotte, had died while she was still a child, so she was given away in the ceremony by her uncle, Frederick. Here we can see the bridal party, which includes Mary Anne, Edith's grandmother (in the striped dress), and her sisters, Constance Charlotte and Mary Anne, who were among the eight bridesmaids in attendance.

63

**Taddington, wedding of Louisa Anne Bramwell, 1912**
Louisa Bramwell married Norman Thomson, originally of Manchester but then
of Shanghai, at St Michael's Church, Taddington, on 17 August 1912. The bride
is seen here carrying a bouquet of dark red roses, making her way to the church
with her father, Samuel Bramwell of Taddington Hall. A reception was held
in a marquee on the lawn at the hall, and villagers and employees from the
firm of Messrs Bramwell, Fern and Co., produce brokers, shared in the
occasion. After a motoring tour, the couple were to leave England for
their new home in Shanghai.

**Bradbourne, Phoebe Rowland, *c.*1900**
At the time her photograph was taken, Phoebe
Rowland would have been living as a widow with
her son Samuel Eyre, a gardener, and his family.
Born in Bradbourne in 1817, Phoebe Rowland
had probably lived in the village all her life. The
daughter of Francis Eyre, a labourer born in
Bradbourne, it would seem that her son Samuel was
actually illegitimate and that she had another
illegitimate son by a different father. She ended up
marrying James Rowland in 1855, who was a cordwainer,
or shoe-maker. James had died in 1888 and been buried in
Bradbourne churchyard, where Phoebe would join him in 1906.

Mr R. Mee, DCHQ006632

### Cromford, former butler and cook at Willersley Castle, c.1925

William Mee worked as a butler to Frederick Arkwright at Willersley Castle, and Ellen Walters was a cook there. While they were living in the household, they began courting, which, as servants, was something they had to do surreptitiously. Once they had taken the momentous decision to marry, they had to leave their employment at Willersley, as demanded by the strict social conventions in country houses at that time. On getting married in 1874, they used their savings to buy the Bell Inn nearby, which remained in the family's hands for over 50 years.

### Bakewell, almshouses, with church behind, c.1903

Here are the old Almshouses on South Church, which stand in the shadow of the parish church of All Saints. The Almshouses had been established in 1602 to provide accommodation for four elderly, poor and single men. In the early 20th century they were providing the same service for local characters glorying under such nicknames as 'Snuffy Tom', 'Jog me eye' and 'Poet Roe'. The sender of this card has written a few lines in the small area of space on the front left for messages, as people then were only supposed to use the back to write the receiver's address.

DCHQ01221

**Matlock Green, old people of the almshouses, *c.*1904**

Before the introduction of state pensions and the welfare state in general, poorer people faced the prospect of old age with no little dread. The spectre of the workhouse loomed for many, especially for those who had not earned enough to provide for the time when they were too infirm to work. Charity was often the saviour for some, and here we can see the lucky residents who lived in the six houses built by Margaret Harrison 'to provide rest for the aged poor'. Apart from the free accommodation, they each had a weekly allowance of 6 shillings.

**Thornbridge Hall, stableyard, *c.*1920**

Here we can see the servants having some fun, moving a giant stuffed bear about. This was the sort of trophy accessory that country houses used to acquire then, and the owner of the Hall, George Jobson Marples, would no doubt have revelled in talking about it to his many visitors, especially as he was a keen sportsman. It would have been ideal, of course, had it been the master of the house himself who shot the beast. The bear was unlikely, at any rate, to have been the bag of one of his regular shooting parties in the Hall grounds.

Ernest A. Smith, DCHQ00084

**Thornbridge Hall, Mrs Boot in the morning room, c.1931**
The Hall and its estates were willed by the bachelor George J. Marples on his death in 1929 to his 'lady friend', Dorothy Ethel Green, who had to take the name of Marples. She decided not to keep the estate and sold it all to Charles Boot, another successful Sheffield businessman who had taken over the running of the hugely successful construction company founded by his father, Henry. Charles bought the Hall and the Thornbridge estate in 1931 and we can see his wife, Bertha, in the oak-panelled splendour of the morning room.

DCHQ00630

**Parwich, house and garden, c.1910**
This house is called the Fold and is situated in the centre of the picturesque village of Parwich. The Victorian wing was added to the 18th-century house, considerably altering the size and character of it with a kitchen, dairy and cheese store. It was the home of the Swindell family, who built on the land that had been used in ancient time to enclose sheep. This picture would have been taken at the time when the Fold was the property of Mr and Mrs Greatorix and two nieces, the Miss Gadsbys, who opened it up as a guest house.

**Matlock, Dimple Farm, with people outside, c.1912**

This fine house was bought in 1903 by Joseph Allen, whom trade directories described as a 'farmer and haulage contractor'. Having originally started with horse-drawn carriages, he was one of the first in the area to invest in motor cars, recognising their potential as taxi vehicles. Here the lady of the house stands proudly by the entrance porch, wearing an enormous wide-brimmed hat which, with her hair piled up on top, seems to hover over her head. This stone house dates back to at least the 16th century, as confirmed by tree-ring evidence taken from beams and rafters.

**Taddington, family outside cottage, c.1930**

A family stand outside the Fernery, a traditional stone-built house on the Main Road, apparently one of the few in Taddington that faced east. The young girl is Jean Dicken, the granddaughter of Mary Hambleton (on the right), who was originally from Dove Holes but who had married Orlando, a shoemaker from Taddington. The lady beside her was Mary's sister-in-law, Olive, who had married Benjamin Hambleton, a postmaster and chapel organist at Mountsorrel in Leicestershire. The property would later be the site of a tragedy when a later purchaser, Miss Howe, committed suicide there.

### Castleton, cottage at Goose Hill, *c.*1906

The woman standing outside her home at Goose Hill is Mary Wildgoose, who according to the census of 1901 was a widow aged 69 and living with her son John Thomas. Mary was actually born in Latham in Lancashire, and had married Joseph Wildgoose, a local man born in Castleton, by whom she had a large family. They lived in Hulme, Lancashire, for much of their lives, where Joseph was a linen warehouseman, but she and her son returned to the family's Castleton roots after his death.

### Baslow, thatched cottage, *c.*1955

This is an outside view of Thatch End, which was converted from three cottages into one residence. One of the cottages had originally been that of Mrs Sarah Elliott (see page 70). The appearance of thatch on the roof now seems out of place in the Peak District, but it was actually the principal roofing material for dwelling houses until the 19th century. As the use of grey slate tiles from Wales and Cumbria and heavy gritstone slates increased, thatch was regarded as suitable only for poorer, tenanted properties for which no investment in terms of strengthening works was deemed appropriate.

MRS. ELLIOTT'S COTTAGE, BASLOW.

### Baslow, cottage interior, c.1906

This is one of the few images we have of the interior of a more humble residence in the Peak District, and even this one may not be quite what it seems. This postcard view was taken inside the thatched cottages at Nether End (see page 69), used by a widow, Mrs Sarah Elliott, to house a tea room along one of the walkways into Chatsworth Park. There is a cast-iron range, oil lamps, several items attached to the wall, and a rag rug on the floor, but they would all seem to be there for show.

### Grin Low, lady visiting cottage, late 18th century

Among the poorest homes in the Peak District were the so-called ash houses at Grin Low. They were literally a product of the limestone that was quarried and burned there. Old lime-ash waste tips became hard over time, and dwelling spaces were hollowed out of them to accommodate workmen and their families. They gave the appearance of being underground, especially when covered with grass and weeds, and were warm and well insulated. However, they had little provision for sanitation and were also potentially dangerous, as was found out in 1862 when a similar ash house at Dove Holes collapsed, killing four people.

**Eyam, Plague Cottages, *c.*1910**

These picturesque, much-photographed cottages near the Church have a sinister history, being the site where the first manifestation of the plague outbreak in Eyam occurred. George Viccars, a journeyman tailor, was lodging with Widow Cooper in one of the cottages when a box of cloth material from London was opened. In so doing he unwittingly released plague-carrying fleas among the community and paid the ultimate price by becoming the first fatality in September 1665. The plague lasted for over a year and caused 259 deaths before suddenly ceasing in October 1666.

**Bakewell, family goods being taken away, *c.*1903**

Possessions are being taken away from a house in Mill Street, now Buxton Road, as a result of the non-payment of rates on a point of principle. The 1902 Education Act had brought denominational schools into the state system, which meant that they were financed by the rates. Nonconformists claimed it was unfair on them to have to pay for Anglican schools, and the National Passive Resistance Committee was formed to organise opposition against it. Goods were seized in lieu of the unpaid rates and sold at auction, but they were often bought by sympathisers and returned to their owners.

71

Julie Bunting, DCHQ000899

### Peak Forest, Old Dam pump, 1944

This is one of the three village pumps that the village of Peak Forest possessed in the days before water arrived through pipes. This particular pump was situated in the hamlet of Old Dam and provided water for cattle that were brought down by nearby farmers. We can see that these residents used their initiative to get water to their houses, filling a large drum set on a trolley with old pram wheels, to save journeys to and fro. They also used to collect rain water at their houses, an act of expediency well before the idea of environmental recycling.

### Ashbourne, Salt Alley, mid-20th century

This photograph appeared in an edition of the *Ashbourne News Telegraph* in 1981 under the title 'Salt Alley as it was'. Salt Alley lies off the south side of St John Street in Ashbourne, between numbers 48 and 50, next to the Duke of Wellington pub. The red-brick cottages on the right-hand side would have housed several working-class families in what were probably quite cramped conditions. The census returns from 1901 backwards show that the adult residents made their livings variously as shoemakers, tailors, clerks, charwomen and work-hands at Cooper's corset-making factory.

Published courtesy of the Ashbourne News Telegraph, DCHQ000555

**Ashbourne, gentlemen playing cards in garden, *c.*1910**

This was taken in the rear garden at 'Brookside', 58 St John Street, Ashbourne. Four gentlemen of a certain age sit down to play a game of cards, arranged in such a way that all of them can be pictured by their photographer friend, Hans Peter Hansen. One of the card players is likely to be George Edinmore Gather (born in 1850), the owner of the house and the manager of the works on Station Street of Richard Cooper Ltd, which had been manufacturing stays and corsets in Ashbourne since 1855.

# LIFE ON THE LAND

In spite of the temptation of city-dwellers to look on the country landscape as an unchanging rural idyll, the truth is that it has always been subject to change, most of it man-made. Forests and trees have been cleared to bring land into cultivation, dry stone walls have been built to enclose fields of land and even the action of grazing animals means that the landscape is not as natural as one would think.

'The Peakland is very barren and in it much rain falls.' This bold statement of a 1908 directory perhaps does the region something of a disservice. There is only limited grazing for sheep up in the moorlands, but lower down in the valleys the prospects for arable and dairy farming have always been greater. Sheep farming is obviously an important part of the agricultural economy, and several images show various aspects of it such as flocks travelling along country lanes, the washing of sheep in fast-flowing rivers before wool is sheared and the important work of the sheepdog as recognised by participation in sheepdog trials.

This section concentrates on farming practices in the Peak District, giving us an indication of how things used to be done. Even though much of the basic activity remains the same, improvements in technology over the last hundred years have meant that many processes are now heavily mechanised and done with greater speed, if not necessarily greater profit, than before.

Food production has been and always will be the primary purpose of farming and agriculture. These days, however, farming continues to face the prospect of change, and there is much more of a trend towards diversification. Farmers are taking on a wider range of farming activities, explicitly promoting their roles as conservationists in the countryside, and taking up the challenge of providing greater tourist and recreational opportunities.

DCHQ006509

**Castleton, men with sheep at Winnats Pass, 1909**
The life of a shepherd was often difficult, with long days in all types of weather and many miles to cover over rough terrain. Here we can see a couple of men with a small flock of sheep, with a sheepdog lying down on the edge of the trackway. They appear in this book in another photograph, taken near the entrance to Speedwell Cavern. Shepherds did form their own societies, whereby they looked after any stray marked sheep they found, returning them to their owner at society meetings held during the year when reimbursement for their upkeep would be paid.

**Bradwell, sheep on the road, *c.*1900**

This is a scene at the turn of the last century, showing sheep being walked into Bradwell. They are heading southwards from the village of Brough on the road known as Bathamgate, which was believed to be an old Roman road. They have just passed by the New Bath Hotel in an area called Edentree, the site of a hot spring well known for the medicinal purposes of its waters since the Tudor period. By the time of this picture, the hotel's business from the spring had largely fallen away. Edentree is now the site of a caravan park.

**Ladybower, flock of sheep on road, *c.*1950**

For centuries Derbyshire has been an important area for sheep farming. In mediaeval times the monasteries established vast sheep farms on the upland hills and moors. A trade in wool and woollen goods also developed with Yorkshire, passing along the several packhorse routes between the two counties. In the 19th century sheep numbers fell, as the trend moved towards dairying in order to meet the demand for such products from the surrounding industrial areas. Here we can see a flock of sheep as they head along the road next to Ladybower reservoir.

Published courtesy of the *Derby Evening Telegraph*. DCHQ006507.

### Handley Bottom, sheep on road, c.1970

Flocks of sheep are still moved around in much the same way that they have been for centuries, and it is not that rare to encounter them on country lanes or even on A roads, such as here on the A6020 to the north of Bakewell. These are believed to include Derbyshire Gritstone sheep, which originated from the Goyt valley area and were well established as a breed by the end of the 19th century, as recognised by the establishment of the Derbyshire Gritstone Sheep Breeders Society at Bakewell in 1906. Other Derbyshire sheep breeds include the Whitefaced Woodland, the Jacob and the Lonk.

### Ashford in the Water, sheep dipping, c.1960

Before shearing the sheep, it was the widespread custom to wash them first, so that the fleece would be less full of waste and impurities and command a better price when sold. At Ashford in the Water a small stone-walled enclosure was built next to the mediaeval packhorse bridge and the sheep would be individually washed in the fast-running water of the River Wye. It used to be a communal activity, taking place over several days in late May and early June. Demonstrations can still be seen during the well dressing festival in the village.

W.H. Brighouse, DCHQ004242.

**Tissington, sheep dipping, *c.*1980**

'In June wash thy sheep where the water doth run,
And keep them from dust but not keep them from sun,
Then shear them and spare not, at two days anende,
The sooner the better their bodies amend' (Old Rhyme)

Several men are involved here in the dipping, but the one standing in the river had the hardest job. He would have got cold quite quickly, whatever the weather, and holding the sheep underneath the running water like this would have been tiring work. He has just started, as only one sheep has so far got on the nearside bank.

**Ashford in the Water, man shearing sheep, 1934**

Sheep shearing took place from late May into June, after the sheep had been washed in the river nearby. Here we can see that some of the sheep have already lost the fleece they had grown over the past year. They have been corralled together by the river under the watchful eyes of sheep dogs, one of whom is watching the shearing as it happens. It was hard work in the days before mechanical shears, and there were suitable breaks to take a breather and sharpen the instruments. This particular shearing was taking place on 6 June 1934.

Published by permission of the *Derby Evening Telegraph*, DCHQ006506

### Chatsworth, sheepdog event, 1977

Sheepdog trials originated in Derbyshire at Longshaw. These are claimed to be the oldest trials in the country following the formation of the Longshaw Sheep Dog Trials Association in 1898. They soon became very popular and grew from a small gathering of shepherds and farmers into an event which received nationwide attention. Sheepdog trials are also held at Bamford, Hope, Dovedale, Hayfield and Chatsworth. The event which took place in April 1977 is featured here, showing the champion sheepdog, Spot, with his owner, Stan Hodkinson from Priestcliffe, and another sheepdog trial expert, Chris Furniss.

### Dovedale, sheepdog trial, 1979

'There is no good flock without a good shepherd and no good shepherd without a good dog' (Dovedale Sheepdog Trials programme). Sheepdog trials are intended to test the skill of dog and handler in situations similar to those they meet every day in their work. Border collies are bred to be working sheepdogs, and they may cover many miles when gathering in the sheep. Qualities of intelligence, stamina and obedience are looked for in them. Held in August, the annual Dovedale Sheepdog Trials take place over two days, and here we can see Chris Furniss with his dog, Mick.

Published courtesy of the *Derby Evening Telegraph*, DCHQ006502

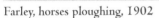

**Farley, horses ploughing, 1902**

Ploughing has taken place for many centuries, and its purpose has remained much the same in all that time, being to turn the soil over so that seed can be sown. Horse ploughing calls for natural ability in ploughmen, as well as good technique learned over time. An experienced ploughman would expect to receive extra remuneration for his skills. The plough is being drawn by a pair of draught horses, whose qualities of strength and stamina were bred especially for the physical demands of this type of heavy farm work. This particular photograph is believed to have been taken at Farley Farm.

**Rowsley, ploughing contest, c.1900**

Ploughing matches were first held in the mid-19th century, with one being recorded at Mickleover in 1843. Pairs of shire horses were decorated for the matches with polished horse brasses, straw plaits in their manes and ribbons in their manes and tails. The purpose of the matches was to encourage high standards and skills in ploughing, but they were also a social occasion for the local community. Some matches still continue, such as those of the Brailsford & District Ploughing & Hedge Cutting Society (founded 1895), whose annual match is held on the first Wednesday in October.

**Manifold Valley, ploughman and team, *c.*1940**

This photograph is believed to show Herbert Wood at Beeston Tor Farm in the Manifold Valley. Howard Davison of Ashover remembers horses being used for ploughing. 'A good pair of horses they'd know what to do on their own. You see, they knew the command, to turn either left or right when they came out at the end of a furrow. It was "ov" and "gee," one word meant turn right and the other meant they turned left. And they didn't need to use the reins to turn 'em. They'd turn with this command. And of course they stopped when you said "Woah".'

**Rowsley, shire horses with wagon, early 20th century**

'Derbyshire has long been famous, and ranked next after Leicestershire, of all the English Counties, I believe, for its stout, bony, clean-leg'd breed of work-horses, principally of a black colour.' So wrote John Farey in 1817 in his *General View of the Agriculture of Derbyshire*. These particular horses are pulling a waggon geared for 'three singles'. They can be identified as shire horses not only by their sheer size, but also by their lower legs, covered with white feathery hair. The horse at the front, in particular, has all the physical characteristics of its kind, with a broad forehead, thick neck and muscular body.

**Farrier, c.1900**

Blacksmiths who deal only with the shoeing of horses are now generally known as farriers. In the days before vets, the farrier would have been an unofficial horse doctor, with his working knowledge of the anatomy of horses and their lower legs in particular. He makes the horseshoes when needed, as well as the nails to attach them. An important part of his job is to literally keep the horses' hooves in good trim. Here, the farrier is resting the hoof on a tripod and has a pair of nippers and a small hammer to do some trimming.

**Brierlow Bar, tractor with farmer and two girls, 1945**

World War Two brought a dramatic decline in the use of horses for work in agriculture, with a corresponding increase in farm machinery. It was essential to bring more land into arable cultivation quickly to increase food production. Tractors had been used for a while, but their numbers now rocketed. There were 46,500 tractors on farms in England and Wales in 1937, and by 1946 the number was 203,400. Here we can see the farmer on his tractor with two young passengers, at Brierlow Bar in the parish of Chelmorton, on 19 June 1945.

Mr R. Litchfield. DCHQ006622

## Matlock, tractors at Megdale, c.1950

Megdale Farm used to be situated close to the old Cawdor Quarry in the Matlock Bridge area. It had been a dairy farm, with some arable land as well. By the time this photograph was taken it was no longer viable for people to live in the actual farmhouse, as quarrying had encroached so close to it. It was demolished later when in a ruinous state. Charles Wildgoose owned the land at the time. One of his sons, Billy or Freddy, is driving the Ferguson tractor in the foreground.

W.H. Brighouse, DCHQ006515

## Glutton Bridge, general view with tractor, 1972

A typical White Peak scene, showing limestone rocks on the hills, a limestone wall and a couple of field barns. Many such field barns are scattered across the Peak District. They were originally built to shelter animals and to store crops, hay and farm implements. Although many of them have fallen into disrepair, some have been converted into camping barns. This particular photograph was taken in July 1972 at Glutton Bridge, which is in the parish of Hartington Upper Quarter. The placename Glutton has nothing to do with the eating habits of any of the locals, but derives from an ancient Anglo-Saxon name.

**Bradwell Dale, tractor loaded with hay, c.1960**
The basic design of the tractor is simple, primarily consisting of a chassis, two large wheels for power, two smaller ones for steering, the engine and the seat for the driver. Nowadays, drivers are more likely to be enclosed in a cab for health and safety reasons rather than sitting in the open, but the tractor design has hardly altered since they first appeared over a hundred years ago. This particular tractor pulling its heavy load of hay was apparently a Fordson, a light, sturdy and relatively cheap model, developed by the same Henry Ford who revolutionised the mass-production of motor cars.

**Brough, with horse and hay cart, early 20th century**
It was essential to cut, dry and store hay to provide a winter feed for cattle and sheep. In the Peak District, haymaking generally began around the beginning of August, although it could happen earlier on the lower ground. The hay was cut by hand with a scythe or by horse-drawn mowing machines, which started to appear in the 1850s. It would then be turned to allow drying, gathered with rakes, then made into haycocks. These were tossed into the cart and made into a haystack at the farm.

**Rowsley, cutting the hay, early 20th century**

This photograph shows a horse-drawn mowing machine in action at East Lodge. An old farmer, Howard Davison, recalls haymaking: 'The grass cut in early June takes longer to dry, because it's so full of sap. They used to say there was nothing like some good June hay. It was full of nourishment, young grass. We used to try and get some June hay if we could. But it took such a lot of killing at that time because there was so much sap in it. Ah. When you got towards the end of July, the grass was starting to go dead.'

**Ashover, haymaking, *c.*1930**

Howard Davison is the boy with the dog here, and recalls haymaking at Dale Bank Farm, Milltown: 'After you've mown with the horse-mower, there's always a bit left round the outside that you can't mow with a mowing machine. So, in those days, that mustn't be left. It had got to be cut. So we went with a scythe and we hobbed it out. And that's where the term "hobbing out" comes from. Mowing the grass round the outside of the field with a scythe, that the mowing machine can't touch.' Two horses were needed to pull the fully laden haywain.

**Ashover, harvesting, 1930**

Harvesting is being done at Hilltop Farm with a machine known as a self-binder. Before the horses and binder went into the field, the edges of the field to about eight feet would have been scythed by hand to prevent damage by the horses and machinery, and the corn gathered into sheaves and tied by hand. The binding machine harvested the rest of the corn field, tying it into sheaves as it cut. It reduced time spent doing everything by hand, but it would ultimately be replaced by the combine harvester. These particular horses were called Beauty and Bess.

**Matlock Moor, harvesting, c.1930**

We can see here a team reaping corn at harvest-time. The horse-drawn reaper would cut the corn and collect it up for binding by a man at the back. Behind the machine several men would follow, bundling the corn up and binding it into sheaves, which were left to dry in the field before being taken away to the farmyard. The young man is holding the handle to release the corn onto the ground for binding. The old man is dressed up in an old-fashioned way, with his knee breeches and leggings, almost as if it were winter.

### Threshing, late 19th century

Threshing is the process by which seed is removed from the stalks of cereal crops. It all used to be done by hand, using a flail on a threshing floor. This way was long and arduous, but the invention of appropriately designed machinery soon rendered it redundant. This threshing machine is powered by a steam engine, with water supplied from a tank. We can see the wheel which turned the belt running from the engine to the thresher. By the time of World War Two combine harvesters were increasing in popularity. These were machines which cut, threshed and cleaned the corn, all in one operation.

### Bakewell Show, judging Blue Albion cattle, 1929

It is appropriate that there is a picture of this type of cattle from the annual Bakewell Show, as Blue Albions were a Derbyshire breed that originated in the Bakewell and Rowsley area and were also known as Bakewell Blues. They were bred from Welsh Black cattle and white Shorthorn bulls for beef and milk. In 1920 the Blue Albion Cattle Society was formed, publishing the first set of standards. As a breed they had one significant drawback, in that blue-roan animals did not produce the same coloured cattle as offspring. They had lost much of their popularity by the middle of the 20th century.

**Winster, street scene with farmers and cattle, *c.*1900**

This particular photograph is taken from the top of East Bank, looking down on a cattle market which used to be regularly held there. It is close to the site of the Market Hall and Rock Field, which was where the cattle for sale used to be held temporarily and pastured. People would travel several miles to buy and sell livestock here, such as a Mr G. Wilson, who successfully took his bull from Beeley (a journey of about six miles) to be sold in June 1865, as mentioned in *A Victorian Farmer's Diary* by William Hodkin.

**Ashford in the Water, boy with pail, *c.*1890**

This photograph shows a boy carrying a pail up Cross Hill in the village of Ashford in the Water. Children on dairy farms learned how to milk at an early age. John Heathcote learned on his grandfather's farm at Brassington. 'I were about seven year old and I learned to milk with a stone, earthenware jam jar and one hand. But I soon learned to milk properly with bucket and stool and that. Yes, best job, finest thing I ever learnt, farming. Nearly broke me heart when I packed it up.'

Julie Bunting, DCHQ006900

### Rowsley, delivery of milk, c.1900

In the country children generally had to work hard and had many chores to do. Millie Ablett remembers her task at around age 14. 'I used to take milk round. It was in individual cans, pint cans and quart cans and four pint cans. I used to have four or five in each hand. I used to have one or two "depots" where I used to leave them to ease the load, so I didn't have to keep going back home to refill the tins. I used to have four pints in the big one and then start pouring them out.'

### Cromford, man with pails, 1936

A traditional yoke is being worn to carry pails. This sort of image is more usually associated with maids who used to milk the cows and carry the produce themselves, but as we can see in this picture it could be used for carrying other things as well. Milkmaids would usually wear a neckerchief to shield the neck and shoulders from the chafing of the yoke, but in this case the man has his very high collar on. This photograph was one of a number taken on holiday by a camper who was staying at Castle Top Farm in Cromford.

DCHQ006518

88

**Edale, woman on lane near farmstead,** *c.*1900

C.B. Fawcett made a geographical study of Edale in 1916 and found that it was mainly an agricultural and pastoral area, with a large number of comparatively small-size farms. 'Life in this valley down to two or three generations ago was remarkably simple.' Before the area was opened up by rail and road, the isolated community had been self-sufficient, living off their livestock and home-produce of oats, vegetables and root crops, using peat for fuel. Fawcett's conclusion, however, was that 'such a district of poor soil, irregular surface and cool, moist climate, is evidently suited rather for forestry than for agriculture.'

**Tansley, pig slaughter,** *c.*1900

It was common for villagers to keep a pig, fattening it on scraps and leftovers boiled into a swill. It was not always easy for the owners to slaughter the pig themselves, so a 'pig sticker' could be asked to do the actual killing. It was done on a bench outside, with the blood being caught in a bucket for use in black puddings. The meat was salted for saving or use in meat pies, and some of it was shared among people who had provided scraps for the pig. The family members pictured here are from the Marsh family of Foxholes.

**Rowsley, forest clearance with horses, *c.*1900**

This work was very hard indeed and labour intensive. Trees would have had to be chopped down, and all their root systems cleared from the ground. Here there are two horses being used to pull logs away, led by a handler, and several men are involved in fence building. It has been worked out from the Domesday Survey of 1086 that about 30 per cent of Derbyshire was woodland. By 1949 this figure had dwindled to four per cent. According to *Kelly's Directory* of 1908, 'There are not many great woods, but poles and other timber are grown for the mines'.

**Youlgreave, farming scene, 1907**
It is not entirely clear what is going on here. A draft horse stands by ready for action, but the men seem in no immediate hurry to provide it, probably thinking about the best way of carrying out whatever it is they hope to achieve. It has, nonetheless, engaged the attention of a woman and a boy who have stopped to have a look over the wall. They are in Lathkill Dale, close to the River Lathkill, which flows through the parish of Youlgreave, meeting up with the River Bradford at Alport.

**Hartington, empty dewpond near Crowdecote, 1999**
Known locally as 'meres', many circular dew ponds are to
be found on the limestone hills in the Peak District, man-
made structures which had become quite common by the
19th century. They were built to provide a ready water
supply for sheep and cattle. Lined with lime and clay and
then covered with gravel, ash or broken stones, the ponds
are able to hold water. Although their name would
suggest that dew is the primary source of water, it tends
to be the rain and surface water which fills the ponds. As
we can see here, they did not necessarily always retain
their water.

**Ashbourne Hall, gardener with wheelbarrow, c.1910**
This photograph is believed to have been taken in the
grounds of Ashbourne Hall. Gardeners worked long hours
(a 12-hour day was common) under the strict discipline of
the head gardener. The garden apprentice, or 'crock boy',
progressed to improver journeyman, then journeyman, and
foreman. Gardens were labour intensive. On a large estate
the kitchen garden alone was tended by 20 to 30 men. The
Hall had become a hotel in 1901, but that particular
enterprise ended after World War One, and the grounds
became the site of a public park and the Memorial
Gardens.

Watford Museum, DCHQ005835

**Matlock, St Andrew's Home kitchen garden, 1904**
This was the kitchen garden of the St Andrew's Home, an orphanage for boys. It would have been an invaluable asset for such an institution, allowing them to grow their own herbs, fruit and vegetables. It was much more common then for people to grow their own than to buy in produce. It certainly looks as if the old gentleman here would have plenty of ground to take care of and no shortage of work to do. No doubt some of the boys would have been drafted in to help him when required.

**Cromford, caravan occupied by Mr Goodwin, 1951**
There was a long-running dispute between Mr Maurice Goodwin, who lived in the caravan on Porter Lane, Cromford, and Matlock Urban Council. This photograph was taken on 3 March 1951. He was later summoned by magistrates in February 1952 for continuing to use the land in contravention of a court order. Mr Goodwin said that he would gladly leave if he could find other accommodation, but there were 500 names on Matlock Council's housing list and he had 'no chance whatever' of obtaining a house. He was fined £10 and, in addition, the caravan was broken up by court order.

DCHQ000769

**Matlock, Hearthstone Farm, 'tossing the sheaf', *c.*1960**
'Tossing the sheaf' was a form of competition which developed out of one of the activities that farmers and agricultural labourers did as part of their work. The idea was to throw a sheaf of hay high in the air with a pitchfork, usually over a bar. The sheaf itself is difficult to see here, but can be made out towards the top of the tree. This is taking place at a Young Farmers' Club ploughing match at Hearthstone Farm. These clubs developed in the 1920s to provide opportunities for young people in the countryside to socialise with others.

93

**Stoney Middleton, view, *c.*1900**

Although Stoney Middleton was an area with a long history of lead mining activity, most of the workers were actually involved in agriculture at this time, many of them being tenant farmers of the Duke of Devonshire and Lord Denman. It was common for many farmers to have supplementary trades, working as butchers, shopkeepers or the like. According to *Kelly's Directory of Derbyshire and Nottinghamshire*, 1908, 'the village has a very picturesque appearance, some of the houses being situated one above another on the ledges of rock, and others at the foot of the overhanging precipices, which rise above them'.

**Tissington, villagers by pond, *c.*1950**

Tissington is, by any standards, an attractive place, described by one writer, without exaggeration, as 'a picture of exquisite beauty'. This photograph shows an almost idyllic scene of the archetypal English village, as a couple chat at the bottom of their garden with a neighbour who has stopped his own gardening work to take part. Behind is the village pond, also known as the Duck Pond, and the old school. This was built in the Elizabethan style in 1837 with the money of the FitzHerbert family of Tissington Hall, but was closed and eventually turned into a tea room in 1979.

# MARKETS AND SHOPS

Many towns and villages in the Peak District have had their own market or fair, even surprisingly small places. In the past it was considerably more difficult for local residents to travel far to go and buy things, so the markets came to them, offering them the chance to purchase everyday household goods such as pots and pans, or giving farmers the chance to buy and sell their livestock.

Markets often bustled with life, attracting people from far and wide. Apart from the locals, people such as travelling tinkers, peddlers and quack doctors would turn up to try and sell their wares. Occasionally there would be hiring fairs, where people would offer themselves up to be taken on as a shepherd, labourer or the like. In a town like Bakewell the market became a indispensable part of its economic life, with strong efforts being made only recently to keep it a vital force there.

Villages and towns also had their own shops to help meet the demands created by people's basic needs. There were all sorts of different shops, providing a wide variety of different services. Most places had their own butchers, grocers, shoemakers and tailors, all people who made their living by directly serving their local community.

In the second half of the 20th century there would, of course, be a revolution in shopping that would turn the whole retail world upside down. Supermarkets totally changed the way we shopped, offering more choices and cheaper products, but often to the detriment of local shopkeepers and farmers. We have seen this process gain further momentum, with the continued development of vast out-of-town shopping malls and retail parks.

There are, however, signs that there is something of a return to the old ways. As people become more and more aware of the environmental impact and false economy of importing produce from the other side of the world, pressure from the consumer has meant that recent initiatives such as the farmers' market and the call for locally sourced products have contributed to a growing call for a change in the retail culture.

**Bakewell, the Old Market Hall, mid-20th century**
The Old Market Hall is an early 17th-century stone building, where traders used to display their wares. The Bridge Street side was built with open, wide arches which were blocked up and filled with windows in the 18th century. Having been turned into a Town Hall in 1827, it was then used for several local government purposes, having had courtrooms, rating offices and a library at one time or another. It has also found itself used at times in other ways, accommodating a washhouse, restaurant and two shops. It now serves as a Tourist Information Centre for the Peak District National Park.

Market House, Winster.

### Winster, Market Hall, c.1955

The Market Hall is believed to date back to the 17th century. It stands almost in the middle of the main street in Winster. As the fortunes of the market declined in the 19th century, the building itself fell into a dilapidated state. It became so unsafe that the upper storey had to be taken down in 1905 and rebuilt. The restoration, using as much of the old material as possible, was undertaken after consultation with the National Trust, who went on to acquire the hall as its first Derbyshire property in the following year. It now houses a Tourist Information Centre.

### Ashbourne, market day, c.1910

The photograph shows a typical market day, traditionally a Thursday in Ashbourne, as people wander by the stalls. The town has always been a trading centre, having been granted its market charter during the reign of Henry III in 1257. As well as weekly general markets, there were also individual ones to buy and sell cheeses and horses, and others held to mark special occasions. The Market Place was often a scene of entertainment on those days, with the likelihood of a sizeable audience. The building to the right is the Town Hall, built in 1861.

### Ashbourne, market day, c.1955

This is another view of the Market Place showing the stalls out on market day, with a number of vehicles parked up. To the right is the George and Dragon Pub, with its distinctive carving set high above the main door, which depicts the saint slaying the dragon. In the front of it is the monument erected in 1874 to Francis Wright, the wealthy local entrepreneur and builder of Osmaston Manor. To the left is Spencer's Café, earlier known as Spencer's Dining Rooms. This particular family had been bakers and confectioners in the town for many years.

### Ashbourne, Market Place, c.1900

This postcard view is looking into the upper part of the Market Place. Despite the goods in the street, this is not an actual market day, as traders often displayed their products in this way. To the left we can see the sign for Hill's Boots, the business of George Hill and Co. Ltd, and beside it the shops of earthenware dealer John Adin, basket-maker Thomas Gregory and draper Mary Baugh. On the right side the Wright monument stands in front of other shops, and in the distance we can see the tower of St John the Baptist Church.

### Buxton, stalls at Higher Buxton Market, 1937

It turned out late for a town of Buxton's size to actually be granted a market, as it did not receive a royal charter authorising one until 1813. The Local Authority took over the right to hold the market in 1864, when the charter rights were purchased from the Duke of Devonshire. This photograph was taken on 31 July 1937, several weeks after the Coronation of King George VI on 12 May 1937, although the Town Hall in the Market Place still bears the message 'Long Live the King' and has other royal decorations on its front.

### Bakewell, livestock market, c.1960

In 1330 Henry III granted Bakewell the right to hold a 15-day fair and this expanded over the years into a regular livestock market and specialist fairs for different produce. By the end of the Victorian era the livestock market would always take place on a Monday. Eventually permanent pens were set out, and regular auctions began in 1914 when W.S. Bagshaw and Sons conducted them. However, many sales were still done privately, deals being settled with the slap of two right hands and the exchange of sixpence or a shilling luck money, a practice still carried on in recent times.

**Bakewell, sheep auction at the old market, 1996**

This is a photograph showing the old livestock market not long before it moved to the new Agricultural Business Centre on the other side of the River Wye. By the 1990s every Monday meant heavy traffic congestion on the main A6 road, as farmers brought their stock into market. In 1996 the Bakewell Project was set in motion to bring about the redevelopment of this old market site, to be replaced with a supermarket, shops, offices, housing and other buildings. In 1999 the Agricultural Business Centre, where the new market was established, was opened by the Princess Royal.

**Bakewell Showground, *c.*1985**

The Bakewell Show is one of the great annual events in the area, attracting crowds of thousands to the two-day event every August. It was founded in 1819, the brainchild of Wootten Burkinshaw Thomas, who thought a show would be a good way of promoting local farming, which was then in a depressed state. Having been at several venues, it was established at its current 20-acre site in 1926. Here we can see how large scale it is, with a sizeable area for livestock competitions and show-jumping, several marquees, and trading stands with plenty of people milling about them.

### Bakewell, J.H. Nelson & Sons, butchers, 1991

The business was founded in 1842 when Horatio Nelson moved from Manchester to Bakewell. He had premises in Mill Street (which was later renamed Buxton Road) from at least 1857. The business prospered for well over a century and a half, passing down through three generations of the Nelson family. They specialised in pork, slaughtering local pigs on the premises and selling the whole range of products, including joints, pork pies and sausages. They built up an excellent reputation and supplied the Dukes of Devonshire and Rutland. This photograph of John Nelson was taken in June 1991 shortly before he retired.

Published courtesy of the Derbyshire Times, DCHQ005567.

### Hathersage, butcher's shop, 1913

Frederick Walter Redfern was the proprietor of this shop on the corner of Main Road and Station Road from about 1911 to 1925. He is standing on the left, next to all the different types of joints hung up for display outside. The premises have been modernised, but it still apparently survives as a butchers shop, run by the Bowyer family. The legend about this property, now known as Brook Cottage, is that it served as the model for a shop depicted in Charlotte Brontë's *Jane Eyre*, where the heroine attempted to exchange her gloves for a cake of bread after leaving Mr Rochester's home.

DCHQ005692

### Birchinlee, butcher's wagon, *c.*1910

When the project to build the Howden and Derwent Reservoirs was set in motion, a temporary village sprang up in 1901 at Birchinlee to cater for the workers of the Derwent Valley Water Board, known colloquially as 'Tin Town'. As well as the workmen's huts, provision was made for a number of public buildings such as a school, hospital and recreation hall (pictured on the terrace). To the right is the wagon of Jesse Eyre of Bradwell, who travelled in to perform the role of butcher for the community. He can be seen settling accounts with some of the women.

### Matlock, butcher's mobile van, *c.*1925

Here we can see Frank Baldock, who was employed as a pork butcher by the Spendlove family business. He is standing in front of their delivery van, tempting a local tabby cat, presumably with a little bit of meat. Job Spendlove seems to have learned his trade as a butcher in Derby, before setting out on his own in Matlock in about 1906, when he opened premises on Dale Road. He actually died in 1925 when aged only 44, leaving the business to his widow, Ada Spendlove (née Wall), who carried it on for at least another 16 years.

**Buxton, Morten's milk float, c.1907**

The Morten milk business was established by John Morten in 1877. He was originally a farmer of 200 acres in Wormhill. He passed it on to his son, Richard B. Morten, who set up the Buxton Creamery and would one day bring in his own son, John. They based their business on produce from their own farm, in the form of milk, cheese, butter and eggs. At one time they also offered 'nursery milk in sealed bottles'. Here one of their delivery carts is standing in Market Street outside the premises of Walter T. Dicken, hairdresser and stationer, next door to Thornton's Confectioners.

Published courtesy of the *Derbyshire Times*, DCHP00016010

**Calver, Taylor's mobile fruiterer's van, c.1930**

William Taylor began his business in Baslow as a shopkeeper in about 1922. By 1928 he had decided to specialise in fruit and is listed as a fruiterer in local directories, taking his sons into the business later. Here we can see his delivery van doing the rounds in the neighbouring village of Calver. It has stopped outside a house at Lowside, where the deliveryman is talking to its lady owner. In the mean time, a small boy in his hat has planted himself in front of the photographer, almost daring him to take his picture.

Mrs J. Gregory, DCHQ504796

Mr R. Mee, DCHQ005632

**Cromford, Reeds' Store and the Bell Inn, c.1897**

On the left side of the photograph of North Street is the shop of James Reeds and Sons, who were grocers. James had originally been a railway clerk, but had set up his own shop by 1891. Alison Uttley may have been describing Reeds as one of the little shops in the village she remembered as a child, 'each one proudly kept, neat and clean, with ready service, and gossip waiting for the customers' pleasure'. On the right is the Bell Inn, which was then run by William and Ellen Mee, who are standing outside with one of their grandchildren. There is a close-up photograph of the couple taken almost 30 years later on page 65 of this book.

**Buxton, High Street, W. Wood and Sons, grocers, c.1920**

The first reference to a shop in High Street run by a member of the Wood family comes in 1870, when George is described as a grocer there. Under William the business expanded profitably, with another shop opening in Spring Gardens. They offered a wider range of services, such as baking and the selling of wine and spirits, at a time when consumer expectations of what shops could provide had started to rise. The family business was sold in the 1920s, and it would be known by 1928 as the International Tea Co. Stores Ltd.

**Calver, Gill & Sons, grocers, c.1936**

The bunting and flags are out at the shop of William Gill and Sons, family grocers and corn merchants, possibly for the Silver Jubilee of George V in 1935 or the Coronation of George VI in 1937. The Gill family had originally been farmers at Froggatt, and it was William who first set himself up as a grocer and butter dealer at Calver from around 1881. In later advertisements he described himself as a wholesale and retail grocer, draper and general outfitter, as well as a boot and shoe dealer, selling products such as corrugated iron sheets, wire netting, hams, bacon and fresh bread.

**Hathersage, grocers and provision merchants, c.1955**

This is probably the Ramsden family outside their grocery shop on Main Road in Hathersage. Fred is listed in local trade directories as being there from about 1951 to 1969, running a shop and off licence with his wife Evelyn. There is a narrow notice just over the door which could be a licensing sign. In terms of grocers' shops in Hathersage in 1951, this was one of no less than five, but Ramsden's was the only one that also operated as an off licence. On the left the window display is advertising the wide range of Carter's seed packets available for purchase.

104

Published courtesy of the Derby Evening Telegraph. DCHQ006561

### Bakewell, Skidmore's grocery shop, 1982

When Skidmore's shop on Matlock Road in Bakewell closed in 2006 it was the end of an era, as it was the oldest grocery in the town. It had been founded by John Skidmore in 1919. They were well known for their 'home grown' produce, locally sourced. John died in 1946, but his widow continued the business on, later involving her sons, Mike (pictured here) and Graham. The shop was intentionally never modernised and attracted much attention for its licensed display of game hung outside the shop, which eventually fell foul of new regulations.

### Hope, 'Hope Chest', interior, 1987

The shop known as 'Hope Chest' was opened in 1980 by Barbara Wilkinson, Sheila Reynolds and Pauline Payne. Their aim was to set up the village shop on Castleton Road as a real alternative to the large retail stores, making personal service the top priority. A success with locals and visitors alike, it prospered and expanded, almost into a mini department store. It has offered a variety of different goods and services, having had a small café restaurant, delicatessen, bookshop with sections for health food, upmarket gifts, high quality women's clothing and even homeopathic remedies.

Published courtesy of the Derbyshire Times. DCHQ005600

## Buxton, International Stores, 1974

This store, on Spring Gardens, was part of the countrywide business called International Stores, which later became Gateway and is now known as Somerfield. This type of store was built on the concept of self-service, which had originated in America but took hold in Britain in the 1950s and 1960s. The queue here is for bread during the Bakers' Union Strike, a nationwide dispute by December, which affected the large supermarket chains quite badly. The site of this store is now occupied by the retail outlet Argos.

## Bakewell, Allen's draper's shop, 1899

Fred Allen was still establishing his drapery and haberdashery business on Rutland Square at the time the picture was taken. Drapers were originally makers and sellers of woollen cloth, and their shops sold all types of textile goods. A full page advertisement in Grattons's *Bakewell Almanac of 1907* gives some indication of the vast range of goods sold or made to order, including dress materials, suits, gloves, corsets, hats, caps, collars and cuffs, skirts, blankets, lace curtains and even 'wool and feather beds made on the premises'. Here we can see a young man ready to deliver an order on his tricycle.

**Buxton, Milligan's Drapery, 1911**

John Milligan founded the business in 1846 and was succeeded by his son, Edward C. Milligan, in 1872. Despite the rapid growth of city department stores, small towns such as Buxton were still able to offer the quality of product and individual service that attracted a loyal clientele. The *Buxton Guides* for 1922 and 1929 have full-page advertisements describing themselves as leading fashion drapers, selling ladies' gowns, costumes, blouses, millinery and dressmaking services. This particular picture shows the decorations at the shop on the Crescent for the celebrations of the Coronation of King George V on 22 June 1911.

**Buxton, 'Millers' Confectioners, interior, c.1938**

The business first appeared as 'Millers' Confectioners in *Kelly's Directory* of 1925 and continued to be listed as such until 1941, when they were included as a café and restaurant. The idea of having a café in the store grew out of the practice of bakers and confectioners serving tea and cakes to regular customers. This would seem to be the case with this business in Spring Gardens, where we can see the sign for visitors to go upstairs for the café. Its 1974 advertising emphasised it was still in family ownership. There is currently a Millers Restaurant at 25 Spring Gardens.

**Buxton, Grandjeans, confectioners, 1938**

Marcel Grandjean was the proprietor of the confectioners Grandjeans Ltd, at 65 Spring Gardens, a business first listed in *Kelly's Directory* of 1936. From the window display it is apparent that handmade chocolates were the main items the shop sold. It required particular skills to make them to the high standards expected of such shops, such as 'conching', when the chocolate was mixed vigorously and cocoa butter added. Although the process was time-consuming and expensive, as a consequence the chocolate it produced had a texture and quality which machines were not able to match.

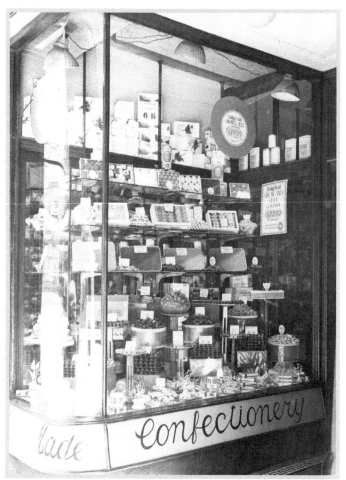

**Bakewell, 'Old Original Bakewell Pudding Shop', mid-20th century**

The property was built in the 17th century and is one of the long low properties that used to be typical of Bakewell's central area and survived the town's later redevelopments. For much of the 19th century the property belonged to confectioners and was run by the Rose family and then the Wilsons. A certain mystery surrounds the origins of the famous pudding itself, with much dispute over the ownership of the original recipe. There are also several stories about its 'discovery', most of which involve cooks at the Rutland Arms Hotel misunderstanding instructions with beneficial consequences.

BKL 100     The Old Original Bakewell Pudding Shop, Bakewell

## Bakewell, 'The Largest Bakewell Pudding', 1987

At the time this was claimed to be the biggest Bakewell Pudding ever made. It contained 210 eggs, a gallon of jam, 300cwt of flour and 100cwt of sugar and almonds. It was made by the 'Original Bakewell Pudding Shop' for the Festival of National Parks and is pictured here in their window display. The Princess of Wales cut the first piece at the event and further slices were sold, raising £610 for Dr Barnardo's, her nominated charity. The Festival was held to celebrate the existence of National Parks, the Peak District Park being the first one designated in 1950.

## Ashbourne, Smith and Sons, wine merchants, *c.*1945

This typically Georgian fronted building at 36 St John Street was the shop of Smiths and Sons, wine merchants. The family business seems to have been going since at least 1846, when Samuel Smith is recorded as a wine and spirit merchant. John Smith continued the trade in about 1852, during the years when he is also described as an agent selling Guinness extra stout ale. His sons were taken into the business from at least 1864 onwards. The site is still concerned with the same line of business, now being known as Smith's Tavern, an award-winning public house.

**Bakewell, Thompson's chemist's shop, *c.*1900**

This picture shows the shop of John R. Thompson in King Street. He was listed in *Kelly's Directory* of 1900 as a chemist, grocer and agent for W.A. Gilbey Ltd, wine and spirit merchants. Versatility was a feature of many shops operating in small towns at that time and Thompson certainly had a diverse range of products. Among the items sold alongside the alcohol and medicines were sheep dip, oil paints, gunpowder and ammunition. John died in 1903, but the business was carried on by his wife Ellen until 1928. The shop continued as Thompson's Drug Store after that date.

**Buxton, Shaw Bros, ironmongers, May 1931**

Ironmongers were initially just retailers of goods made specifically out of iron, but later took on the sale of similar goods made out of other metals. As the demand for a wider range of domestic items increased over time, they became sellers of many different types of consumer goods in hardware shops. Also known locally as the Household Stores, Shaws were a good example of such a shop, selling pots, pans, buckets and spades, as well as other garden equipment, glassware and china. This photograph was taken in front of their shop in Market Street on 7 May 1931.

### Hope, the smithy, 1932

The smithy was situated on the Main Road, next door to the entrance to the cattle market. The blacksmith used to be a very important member of any small community, being able to turn his hand to all sorts of things. In his forge he would make horseshoes, plough share blades, wrought-iron gates, tools and cooking utensils. He could be called upon, as here, to repair all sorts of machinery, using his skill to make any small parts as required, including intricate items like locks. At the time this was taken, Joseph Holme and Sons were the blacksmiths of Hope.

### Buxton, basket makers' shop, c.1880

The ancient craft of basket-making was one that had not been touched by any form of mechanisation at the time this photograph was taken. Using simple materials and tools, it required skilled hands and old-fashioned techniques. This workshop, with its rickety looking lean-to front, belonged to the Raynes family. Established in Spring Gardens by Francis in the 1860s, when he himself was over 65, the business had passed on to his widow, Fanny, in 1876. She carried on for a few more years, but then left the reins to her nephew, George, who kept it going until at least 1925.

**Taddington, Orlando Hambleton, shoemaker, c.1920**
This photograph was taken of the shoemaker, Orlando Hambleton, on the steps of his cottage, known as the Nook. He used it as his workshop, where he specialised in making the clogs worn by the villagers at that time. This was the family business, as his father, Isaac, and his grandfather, Benjamin, appear in census returns as cordwainers or shoemakers, spanning a period of 100 years. Orlando died in 1945 aged 78. The sign above the door is advertising Jones Sewing Machines, so he might have acted as an agent to help supplement his income.

**Baslow, Ellis's fancy goods and souvenir shop, c.1900**
On the left is the fancy goods and souvenir shop owned by Thomas Ellis. The shop would have aimed its market at the tourists who came to the area, particularly those who had arrived to visit Chatsworth, which is within walking distance of the village. It is also likely to have come to the notice of those who would have stayed at the Devonshire Arms next door. Thomas Ellis would later move his premises to a larger shop on the other side of the Devonshire Arms, where he also sold groceries and provisions as well as the fancy goods and toys.

**Matlock, W. Evans & Son, jewellers, c.1910**
The photograph shows William Evans and his son Charles Walter outside their shops at 93/95 Dale Road, Matlock. William had begun his jewellery business in 1850 in Wirksworth. The premises in Dale Road, Matlock were opened in 1893 and have been a constant presence ever since. The son set up as an optician next door to his father's jeweller's shop. Many of their customers probably came via the hydro trade, as they opened further branches up Matlock Bank nearer those establishments. The business passed to the Goward family in 1956, and it has continued to remain a respected part of the Matlock trading community.

**Matlock, Dale Road, c.1920**

Here we can see some of the shops along Dale Road, which was the main shopping thoroughfare in Matlock at that time. It is only in more recent years that the focal point for shopping has moved to the other side of the River Derwent. The Old English Hotel on the right is still going, unlike many of the shops next to it, which have had several different occupiers over time. The types of shops in business then included grocers, linen retailers and fruiterers. This photograph would have been taken in around 1920, showing the road as it was before being tarmacked.

**Buxton, the Colonnade, c.1910**

This is a view of the series of shops called the Colonnade, which were added in 1864 to a complex known as the New Hot Baths. The baths themselves had been added to the side of the Crescent, which can be seen towering above on the right. Part of the redevelopment of Buxton at that time involved the provision of more retail outlets for visitors as well as local residents. People later had the opportunity to do some shopping under the shelter of a cast-iron canopy, which was added in 1909 as part of alterations made by architects Bryden and Walton.

**Bakewell Post Office,** *c.*1905
The new Post Office in Rutland Square was built as part of a wish among the town leaders to move with the times. Not only was it felt that the building then in use was unsuitable for its purpose, but it was also seen as an opportunity to improve the town centre. The narrowness of the road between Charles Crichlow's shoe shop and the Bank had caused many accidents, and by demolishing the shop and setting back the building line, the road would be widened. The new Post Office was erected in 1894, having used monies raised solely by public subscription.

**Buxton, Manchester and County Bank,** *c.*1911
This picture was taken in the days when banks were largely provincial affairs. They had replaced smaller banking institutions founded on the resources of wealthy individuals, which were prone to go under when faced with financial crises. Provincial banks spread the risk, backed up by the resources of other lending institutions. In time, banks would become national institutions, and then global. Here, we can see the interior of the Manchester and County Bank (later taken over by NatWest) on Terrace Road. The photograph shows the manager, Robert Edward Coats, on the left and John Ludlow and Fred Hoyle to the right.

# SPORT AND LEISURE

Here we have identified various ways in which inhabitants of the Peak District enjoy themselves. There may not be the facilities or amenities that large cities are able to provide, but that does not mean there are no options available for people to enjoy themselves here.

Sport figures largely in the images chosen in this section, with various sporting teams lining up to be photographed very much as they are now. In many cases the sporting clothes may be very different, but we can still detect the sense of enjoyment and will to win on many of the participants' faces. One particular local event that we have highlighted is the famous Ashbourne Shrovetide football, which is a proud local tradition, recalling a time when sport was a lot wilder.

There are also a number of images that come under the general term of country pursuits, such as fishing, shooting and hunting. Some might question whether these should be regarded as sport, but there is a counter argument that they may have more right to be called that than activities like football and cricket, which should be more correctly identified as games.

We have also chosen pictures showing other sorts of games, more social perhaps, but not necessarily less competitive. There are images of croquet, tennis and cycling, as well as those of the musical pursuits of brass bands and ballroom dancing, and the downright unusual, such as sending off a Reliant Robin down the river.

Examples of enjoying the outdoor life also appear among the pictures. The landscape of the Peak District has given opportunities for people to indulge in activities such as rock-climbing, potholing and rambling, although these are all surprisingly recent in the general scheme of things, having been taken up only in the last 100 years or so.

**Peak District, 'snap' on the moors, c.1900**
This a fine shot of men who have stopped to enjoy their 'snap' while out in the dales. The word 'snap' originally derived from the mining districts of the East Midlands, meaning the packed lunches miners carried in a snap-tin, but is now recognised as meaning food in general. The man on the left is believed to be James William Puttrell, who was a real pioneer of potholing and climbing in the Peak District. Among his achievements were the first solo ascent of the face of Mam Tor and the first climb out of the top of the Peak Cavern.

### Peak District, rock climbing, *c.*1900

This fine shot shows a man at the end of a rope looking to make his perilous way higher up a gritstone crack. It shows the primitive state of rock-climbing at that time, when climbers did not have the full panoply of appropriate equipment such as harnesses, helmets and modern clothing that they have today. The Peak District was an important area for the development of the sport in the 1890s as people took up the adventurous challenge of conquering its distinctive crags. Unfortunately, the exact location of this photograph is not known.

### Castleton, potholing, *c.*1900

Potholing is an activity that is well served in the Peak District, where the limestone geology lends itself towards the creation of any number of fine cave systems. Here we can see early pioneers as they explore underground in one of those systems in the area around Castleton. One man lurks in the shadows, while another has his leg up on the wall-face to brace himself. He has a candle fixed on his hat, much in the same way as lead miners had done to give them light as they travelled along shafts and worked out the ore.

**Hathersage, ramblers at Stanage Edge, c.1935**
Every year the Peak District attracts thousands of walkers to enjoy the countryside and appreciate the wonderful scenery. Stanage Edge is one of a number of 'edges' in the area, which include Froggatt, Curbar and Burbage, where cliffs of gritstone rock have been exposed to provide spectacular views and vantage points. Stanage, which literally means 'stone edge', is generally reckoned to be the greatest of the edges, with almost three miles of exposed rock, which these days is an immensely popular destination for rock climbers as well as ramblers.

**Castleton, G.H.B. Ward on Losehill, 1945**
George Henry Bridges Ward (1876–1957) was a militant rambler, who campaigned for over 50 years to improve access to the countryside for the general public. On 8 April 1945 his pioneering contribution was marked by a ceremony in which the title deeds of land at Losehill were presented to him by the Sheffield and District Federation of the Ramblers' Association. A further indication of the respect held for him was that the land was renamed Ward's Piece. Here we can see him addressing the crowd of 2,000 ramblers that attended. Shortly afterwards the deeds would be handed over to the National Trust.

**Bathamgate, two walkers, *c.*1935**

Rambling is a most enjoyable way to get about, especially on the moors where there is the opportunity to get away from the stresses and strains of modern life and enjoy some fresh air. Here we can see two hikers, the appropriately named Frederick William Walker and his companion 'T.J.', striding purposefully away from the camera, in their boots and plus-fours and with rucksacks slung across their backs. They are making their way along Bathamgate, which was reputedly an old Roman road, running from Brough to Buxton.

**Buxton, foxhunting in front of the Crescent, *c.*1930**

It looks somewhat incongruous to see horses and hounds in the middle of a town centre, as if the fox has led the hunt a really merry dance. There is, however, a slightly less fanciful reason for the scene. The Crescent was simply one of the places used as a location for meeting up by the High Peak Hunt. Having made their presence felt in the town, they would then set off into the neighbouring countryside to start their hunting in earnest.

**Bakewell, High Peak Hunt, c.1986**

Members of the High Peak Hunt can be seen travelling along Rutland Square, with a pack of beagles and two whippers-in, whose job is to keep the hounds together as a pack. The hunt has traditionally met up in Bakewell before moving off to hunt in the area extending from the town up towards Buxton. They used to hunt hares and foxes until the Hunting Act 2004 came into force. The hunt was originally established in 1848 by William Pole Thornhill of Stanton Hall.

Published courtesy of the *Derbyshire Times*, DCHQ00S560

**Flagg races, 1991**

On Easter Tuesday each year point-to-point races are held on Flagg Moor, attracting thousands of spectators to witness the excitement of horses racing in open country and courageously hurdling stone walls. Point-to-point races originated among the hunting community, as they used racing as a form of training for their horses. Riders would start from a particular place, but could take whatever route they liked to get to the designated finish, usually a clearly defined point in the landscape such as a church steeple (hence the term steeplechase). The races at Flagg have been organised by the High Peak Hunt since 1892.

Published courtesy of the *Derbyshire Times*, DCHQ00S593

**Thornbridge Hall, shooting party, 1911**

This shows a party as they are about to set off from Thornbridge Hall for some shooting. The hall was owned then by George Jobson Marples, a railway company director and financial speculator with a penchant for social climbing (pictured third on the right, with cane). Shooting parties were looked on as perfect opportunities to mix with a 'better class of person', as indicated by the presence of local gentry and two titled ladies on this occasion. There would have been, of course, a whole army of unseen servants, staff and helpers to make sure it all went off well.

**Buxton Station, LMS Railwaymen's Rifle Club, c.1930**

This array of smartly dressed men, including one with an old-fashioned wing-collar tie, exude an air of quiet pride and satisfaction at their achievements, lining up to have their photograph taken with their trophies in front of them. They were members of a team representing the Buxton London Midland and Scottish Railwaymen's Rifle Club. They were photographed on one of the platforms at Buxton Station, with the giant semi-circular fanlight behind them.

### Matlock Rifle Club, 1935

This is another group portrait of successful shooters, as they hold a couple of trophies in the front row. The club, which served Matlock and the surrounding district, had been a successful institution before the outbreak of World War One, but was not resuscitated until 1921. Thirty-three members had joined the armed forces, but six of them had been killed. Some of the members appear to be wearing medals, presumably to do with shooting competitions rather than for military service. The annual subscription for ex-servicemen was 2s 6d, while that for other members was 5 shillings.

### Derwent Bridge, fishing, c.1909

Fishing has long been a pastime enjoyed in the Peak District. Although the influence of Izaak Walton and Charles Cotton has meant the River Dove is better known for angling, good sport has always been possible on the Derwent as well, particularly for trout and grayling. This is an unusual photograph in that it shows the old packhorse bridge at Derwent before the building of Ladybower Reservoir. The bridge was taken down in 1939 with painstaking care, each stone being individually removed and numbered. It would, however, be another 22 years before it was re-erected in its present location above Howden Dam.

304. Derwent Bridge. Near Ashopton.

**Beresford Dale, 'Fishing Temple', *c.*1910**

This building is known as Izaak Walton and Charles Cotton's Fishing House. It is also called the Fishing Temple, and has an inscription carved on its keystone 'Piscatoribus Sacrum' (Latin for 'sacred to fishermen'). It was built in 1674 by the Nottingham architect Lancelot Rolston, at the invitation of the poet Charles Cotton of Beresford Hall. Izaak Walton, who wrote *The Compleat Angler* (subtitled 'The Contemplative Man's Recreation'), had been introduced by his friend to the delights of fishing in the Peak District and the River Dove in particular.

**Ashbourne, Shrovetide football, *c.*1907**

There have been games at Ashbourne on Shrove Tuesday and Wednesday for almost 200 years. The character and nature of the game has remained largely unchanged, and in that time it has survived numerous attempts by the authorities to ban it because of its potential for social disorder. Derby used to have a similar game, but fatalities led to its demise there in the late 19th century. In Ashbourne the tradition grew stronger as time went by, and it is now regarded in a more positive light as an enduring ritual and object of civic pride.

**Ashbourne, Shrovetide football, 1952**

This photograph shows a group of men striving for the ball in Henmore Brook, something usually left to the young or foolhardy. The Brook is an important component of the game, determining not only the make-up of the teams but also much of its location. The teams are traditionally made up of those born north and south of the Henmore, who are known, respectively, as the Up'ards and Down'ards, and the 'goals' are at two mills on the Brook three miles apart. The ball itself is made of stitched leather, deliberately filled with cork so that it can float on water.

**Ashbourne, Shrovetide football, 1981**

The football at Ashbourne is a rare survival of the original form of the sport. It is in the nature of the game for the ball to be swallowed up in the 'hug' and disappear out of sight for long periods of time, as the players sway to and fro. This photograph shows how the term 'football' is not particularly appropriate, as it is more like rugby with all its scrums and mauls. It has been suggested that William Webb Ellis was influenced by fellow schoolboys from Ashbourne when he decided to run with the ball at Rugby School.

**Ashbourne, football team, *c.*1925**
This is an example of the players of the normal, eleven-a-side variety of football in Ashbourne. This is probably a team photograph of Nestlé United Football Club, taken on the sports ground behind the works on Clifton Road, with Nestlé's factory in the background. The players pictured here are: (left to right, back row) J. Hawksworth, S. Siddals and P. Soutar; (middle row) T. Mellor, H. Bennet and F.G. Pugh; (front row) C. Taylor, H. Pegge, Douglas McGregor, W. Redfern and C. Earl.

**Bakewell, football team, *c.*1895**
This photograph was taken outside the house of Robert Orme in Water Street. The Orme family were noted wine merchants and grocers in the town, but they also played a major part in the general development of organised sport in the area. The team shown is Bakewell Town Football Club, which was formed by the amalgamation of two local teams in 1891. The clergyman in the back row is Revd Richard Henry Fuller, who was curate of Bakewell from 1891 to 1897. He played a key role in the running of the club, and was even elected its first club captain.

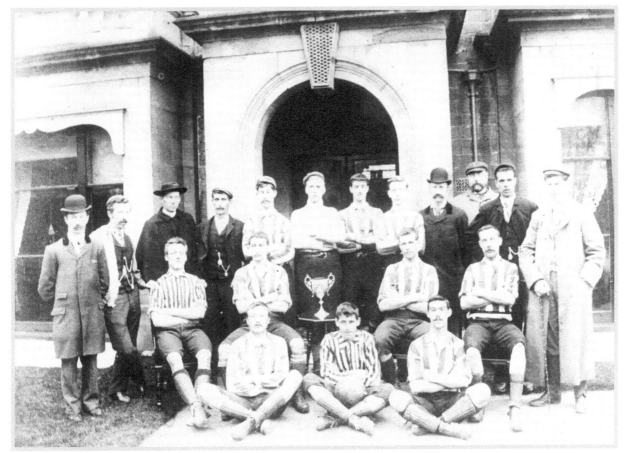

### Darley Dale Wesleyan Football Club, 1909–10

The team are shown outside the Methodist church which gave them their name. The Wesleyan Methodist Church had opened only a few years earlier, in 1902, and, as part of their commitment to attract as many sections of the community to belong to their church as possible, had set up a football team to cater for young men. Other church denominations did the same, and several professional teams can trace their origins back to such evangelical roots, including the Premiership sides Everton and Aston Villa.

### Matlock Junior Football Club team, 1916

This photograph was taken during World War One. Even if the year had not been written on the ball, we could have guessed the period from the presence of the soldier in uniform on the right. Although the playing of football was initially frowned upon by the authorities as a distraction in time of war, the Tommies themselves still regarded the game as an important part of their lives. It is tempting to think that the soldier was a member of the team who had recently joined up and that this photograph was taken as some form of memento.

**Winster, football team, 1921**
This photograph shows a fine array of men who played for the village team of Winster, as they display a trophy and their winners' medals. They had a successful 1920–21 season, winning the senior division of the Matlock and District League. In addition, they were awarded silver cigarette cases, unlikely to be considered an appropriate reward for sporting endeavour these days. The people featured are (back row, left to right): Jack Boam, Harry Walker, George Thomas, Cliff Allwood, Frank Blackwell, Bert Unwin, Alf Heathcote, Bert Marshall; (front row) Herbert Greatorex, Frank Phillips, Jack Twyford, Harold Wild and Donald Greatorex.

### Buxton Rugby Club on Temple Fields, 1970

This photograph shows the hardy souls of Buxton Rugby Club at play on Temple Fields. It may have been one of those days when it was better to find yourself in one of these mauls, with all that body heat of the pack to keep you warm, rather than being stuck out on the wing waiting for the ball to arrive. Although the area has lacked a top-class rugby team, the playing of the game in several local schools has always meant that it has had a presence in the Peak District.

127

**Darley Dale, cricket team, 1895**

The cricket team of Darley Dale were the winners of the Derbyshire County Challenge Cup in 1895. They played in the final against Codnor United at the County Ground in Derby in a two-day, two-innings match, and were awarded the trophy as they had the better of a drawn match. Pictured are (back row, left to right): T. Wright (Hon. Secretary), F. Evans, R.C. Gregory (captain), A.H. Smith (sub-captain), J. Siddal and W.M. Holmes; (front row): Ben Gregory, J. Gregory, C. Pashley, R.B. Wright, H. Gregory, J.J. Wildgoose, J. Wright and W. Gregory.

**Buxton, cricket and rounders teams, c.1900**

This unusual photograph shows a group of ladies and gentlemen mingled together in front of the steps leading up to the cricket pavilion at Buxton. A lady holds a cricket bat, while a gentleman has one for rounders, which may or may not be a conscious gesture of role reversal. The occasion is not known, but we must assume that they were prepared to play either game in mixed teams. The ground, known as the Park, used to be one of the best in the county and was regularly used for first-class games until only a few years ago.

**Bakewell, ladies' cricket teams, 1930**

The picture shows two immaculately turned-out sides waiting for the toss of the coin. They are lined up in front of the new pavilion at Rutland Recreation Ground, which had been paid for by a former president, Stanley Orme, and opened by the Duke of Devonshire only the year before. The teams represented two local cotton-manufacturing works, Progress (on the left) captained by Ena Darnell, and Melso (on the right) captained by Daisy Fisher. Ladies' cricket was not a new phenomenon in Bakewell, as there is photographic evidence of a ladies team in 1896.

**Matlock, tennis players, *c.*1905**

This fine photograph shows a group of young men and women looking very much à la mode. In the Edwardian era tennis was one of the few sports where it was not frowned upon for ladies and gentlemen to take part together. This made tennis clubs very popular places for younger people, who got the chance to mix in a relatively informal, if somewhat socially exclusive, environment. The ladies are wearing lighter white blouses at this time, and they got round the wearing of hats by serving under-arm and avoiding overhead smashes.

**Buxton, tennis courts, c.1910**

These courts were situated in the Pavilion Gardens, and were built in about 1880 for visitors to enjoy the game of lawn tennis. It proved so popular that the Buxton Improvements Company was to run its own 'open' tournament from 1884, even holding an All-England Ladies Doubles Championship before Wimbledon got round to one. The tournament would remain an important part of the Buxton social scene until 1954. At the time this photograph was taken there would have been gravel all-weather courts as well, as they required much less maintenance and were available for longer in the year.

**Grindleford, croquet, c.1908**

A leisurely game of croquet is being played out on the lawn of the Maynards Arms Hotel. As we can see, it was a game which could be played by both men and women, being particularly popular with the latter as it could be played on a truly equal footing. The hotel had not been open long when this picture was taken, as it was only built in 1900. It was named after Sir Richard Lax Maynard, who fought in the Battle of Agincourt in 1415, and its interior décor incorporates battle scenes, mediaeval forms of dress and armour.

### Buxton, cyclists' meeting, c.1880

People gather round a group of cyclists ready to leave for an excursion, starting from the Swan Inn on High Street. Penny farthings were objects of great curiosity, and to have had several such contraptions in the same place would certainly have caused a crowd to gather. As the penny farthing was notoriously unstable (and looked it), it generally attracted only the young or the brave. The invention of the safety bicycle would, however, take cycling on to a totally different level, when all sorts of opportunities in terms of leisure, travel and day-to-day practicality would be opened up.

### Buxton, roller skating rink, c.1905

It had been the Americans who had started the craze of roller skating in the 1860s. In 1876 Buxton was actually one of the very first places in the country to have a roller skating rink. It was built within the Pavilion Gardens, with the dome of the Concert Hall, now known as the Octagon, visible here in the background. In winter the rink would actually be frozen over to allow people to ice-skate and to play curling. In 1906 it would be converted full-time into a curling rink, that particular sport then being at its height of popularity.

**Matlock Lido, c.1945**

It has always seemed somewhat unlikely that one would find a swimming pool open to the elements in the centre of Matlock, but this was the case from 1938 when it was built by the old Urban District Council and opened to the public at the cost of £12,000. A smaller indoor pool was also provided for less hardy souls at one end and a café for refreshments at the other on Bank Road. The complex was on the site of the old Imperial Gardens. In 1972 the decision was taken to provide a roof for the outdoor pool.

**Matlock Brass Band, c.1900**
This is a photograph of the Matlock Brass Band in civvies rather than any uniforms. The age profile of the band is interesting, as there are the youngsters with their cornets and an old-timer with his double B-flat bass. Hopefully, they displayed the perfect musical blend of youth and experience. The person who is third left on the back row is known to be Anthony Holmes, a stone dresser, while the gentleman on the far left of the back row is believed to be Joseph Marsden, butcher and innkeeper, who let the band rehearse at his pub, the King's Head.

**Bakewell Band, *c.*1910**

These are probably members of Bakewell Silver Band posing in their uniforms at the Recreation Ground, together with some friends and supporters sitting on the grass. The band was formed in 1907 at a time when brass bands were very popular and in demand for all kinds of occasions. The band is still in existence and frequently performs locally at shows, festivals and well dressings.

**Buxton, ballroom dancing, *c.*1959**

The photograph was taken inside the octagonal Concert Hall, which was built by the noted architect, R.R. Duke, who was responsible for the design of many fashionable buildings erected in Buxton. The ballroom appeared in 1875, at the same time that the major enlargements of the Pavilion Gardens took place. The band can be seen on stage in the background, and although there seem to be plenty of spectators sitting by the walls, the event is evidently suffering from the perennial complaint of there not being enough suitable male partners.

133

## Pop festival, 1973

Although Buxton is better known for festivals of opera, there were also pop festivals held in the area between 1969 and 1974. The bill in 1973 was headed by the legendary rock-and-roller Chuck Berry, with supporting acts such as Wizzard (fronted by Roy Wood) and Nazareth, the Scottish hard rock group. Also in attendance as DJ was the late John Peel. It actually took place at Booth Farm near Hollinsclough over the weekend 21–22 July 1973. The price for admission was the princely sum of £2, but the music was advertised as being on for over 12 hours each day.

## Bakewell, elephant shot at circus, 1905

During a performance by Lord John Sanger & Sons' Circus at Bakewell, one of their elephants became enraged and started to attack its keeper. Having been calmed down and led out of the arena, it became angry again and started to run amok. At one stage it threatened to literally tear its way through the tent back into the crowd. Fortunately, the rest of the keepers were able to catch hold of it and restrain it in chains. Help was obtained from members of the Derbyshire Yeomanry and Sherwood Foresters, who formed a firing squad to shoot the unfortunate animal.

Lord John Sanger & Sons' Elephant, Shot at Bakewell, May 25th, 1905. Gratton, Photo. (Copyright.)

### Buxton, Punch and Judy show, 1896

This is the stand used by Harry Bailey, a resident of Buxton who frequently put on shows in his home town. Punch and Judy puppet shows were originally entertainment for adults, with a racy edge to them. By the time Mr Bailey operated, they had changed into something which appealed more to children, involving a wider range of characters and a bit more fun, even if they are unlikely to pass any test for political correctness. Here we can see Mr Bailey in the Pavilion Gardens, with an attendant to bang the drum and, of course, Toby the Dog on stage.

### Matlock, Boxing Day Raft Race, 1987

Every Boxing Day the annual Raft Race takes place on the River Derwent. It has continued, since its first appearance in 1962, to attract large numbers of spectators who look forward to seeing what outlandish ideas the participants think up each year. Starting from Matlock Bridge, rafts of varying shapes and sizes wend their way down the river, passing through Matlock Bath as they go, on towards their ultimate destination of Cromford Bridge, a journey of over three miles. It is certainly no mean test of skill on a twisting course, with many difficult stretches of water to be negotiated.

**Matlock Bath, 'Switchback Ride',** *c.*1910

The rollercoaster ride was opened in 1889, making it one of the earliest in England. Although it was only a small ride (about 140 yards in length) and not exactly in the Alton Towers league, it added an extra novelty value for visitors and day-trippers to Matlock Bath. Advertisements of the period even promoted its health advantages, 'a distinctly medical effect upon the Liver', advocating half a dozen rides to reap the full reward. The ride was situated in the Derwent Gardens on the west bank of the river and was run by water power. It was dismantled in 1934.

# TRADE AND INDUSTRY

Although the landscape in the Peak District is decidedly rural, with only a few medium-sized market towns, this does not mean that agriculture is the only form of economic activity that the area has seen in the past, as different forms of industry have also made up a significant part of the local economy.

Lead mining, for example, has had a notable presence in the area, going back at least 2,000 years. Evidence of lead being mined in the Roman period has survived in the forms of ingots, and it is possible that the industry had roots here even earlier than that. Most of the industry was actually undertaken on a small scale, with work often being undertaken by individuals or small partnerships to supplement their farming. Physical reminders of abandoned lead mining works and shafts can still be detected in the landscape.

Quarrying is probably the most successful industrial activity surviving in the area today. The quality of the area's limestone makes it viable for firms to continue to invest in and expand the quarries, in spite of opposition from many on environmental grounds. There are images which show the industry in several stages of its development, as well as the work of stonemasons helping to fashion it for use in buildings.

The Peak District also has sites which hark back to the early days of the Industrial Revolution, when the pioneering factories of Richard Arkwright set it all in motion. The waters of the rivers Wye and Derwent were used to power the machines that made the textiles. Although highly profitable for many decades, the industry fell away in the face of stiff overseas competition.

There have been other sizeable businesses in the area that are represented, such as Nestlé's factory at Ashbourne and the poultry-processing operation of Thornhill's at Great Longstone. Other images in this section, however, depict smaller, more humble concerns, such as the distinctive rope-making works inside the Peak Cavern, the Hartington cheese factory, a Bradbourne carpenter's premises, and the individual photography business of Hans P. Hansen at Ashbourne.

**Sheldon, Magpie Mine, c.1930**

Lead mining in the Peak District was an industry which went back as far as the Roman period, and maybe even before then. Until the 18th century most mining took place on, or close to, the surface, usually in small-scale enterprises, although opening up shafts to find deeper veins of lead resulted in larger mines such as Magpie Mine. The mine suffered fluctuating fortunes, as it faced the various vicissitudes of foreign competition, continual drainage problems and bitter legal disputes. Mining had finished altogether by 1960, but the site is now maintained by the Peak District Mines Historical Society.

**Darley Dale, Millclose Mine, c.1930**
This photograph shows some of the mine's buildings, including the 'Jumbo' engine house near the Warren Carr Shaft. As shafts were sunk deeper the amount of water needing to be pumped out increased. Water was always the biggest obstacle to mining at Millclose and would eventually force its total closure in 1940. 'Jumbo', however, had been one of the most powerful engines in the country in the late 19th century, performing an important job for the mine for over 50 years until new pumping equipment was introduced in the 1920s.

**Darley Dale, Millclose Mine Dressing Plant workers, 1930**
This photograph shows workmen at the dressing plant. Here, the lead ore that had been mined would be subjected to a variety of mechanical processes. The basic aim was to separate the lead ore from the dirt, waste and other minerals with which it had been extracted. This would be achieved by crushing, sieving and washing the ore, which would consequently be of good enough quality for smelting. Pictured at George Potter's Shaft are (left to right): Bill Blackham, Arthur Vardy, Herbert Heathcote, Bert Webster, Les Flint, Thomas Webster, Chris Stone and Harry Taylor.

**Darley Dale, Millclose Mine workers, 1932**
The men shown here were picking table and jig operators, who were employed at the mine when it was operating at the very peak of its production. Extending over a huge area below the surface, reaching depths of 1,000 feet and employing several hundred men, it had become the largest lead mine ever to be worked in Britain. Back row, left to right: Harry Bowmer, Fred Flint, Wilf Spencer, Dick Bond and Edward Stevenson. Middle row: Stan Marshall, Owen Smith, George Kenworthy, Stan Maynes and Charlie Stewartson. Front row: E. Fisher, Harry Goodwin and Harold Boam.

**Middleton Dale, smelting house, 1818**
Once the lead ore had been mined from ground, a process was needed to extract the metal from the ore and this was known as smelting. Having been washed, pulverised and separated from types of rock, the ore was transferred to a furnace, where it was subjected to high levels of heat. This removed any impurities, and the resultant molten lead was then channelled into moulds to solidify into masses known as 'pigs'. The scene was expertly drawn by F.L. Chantrey and engraved by W.B. Cooke. Note in the foreground the pickaxes and shovel, tools symbolic of the lead-mine workers.

**Bradwell, Brunt Mine, c.1900**
This photograph shows a man operating a windlass, known in Derbyshire as 'stowes', or 'a pair of stowes', which is being used to bring up lead ore from a mining shaft. Although this type of equipment was principally meant for ore, at some mines it was also used to wind men down to where they were working and, hopefully, up again when they finished. In the lead mining industry the bucket, made of iron or wood hooped with iron, was known as a 'kibble'. The image is believed to have been photographed at Brunt Mine near Bradwell.

**Matlock Bath, Upperwood Fluorspar Mine, *c.*1890**

Fluorspar is the name by which the mineral calcium fluoride is generally known. Initially regarded as little more than a by-product of the lead mining industry, it became an important commodity in its own right. Aside from its use as a flux in the steel-smelting process, it could also be appreciated just for the way it looked, as a fluorescent, visually attractive mineral. There were several retail outlets dealing in fluorspar ornaments in Matlock Bath at that time, so one can suppose that some of the material mined here at Underwood could have been worked up to make such objects.

**Eyam, Ladywash Mine, *c.*1950**

Originally this mine had been worked for lead ore in the 18th century, but production there had ceased by the end of the 19th century. It did, however, achieve a renaissance with the growth of the fluorspar mining industry. In 1940 it was relined with concrete and worked again for this valuable commodity. The mine had a deep shaft, going down 800 feet, with workings along veins a mile long. Its respite was relatively brief, as its working area began to be encroached upon by other nearby mines, and it was closed again in 1979. The photograph shows the old engine house and chimney.

**Snitterton, Oxclose Mine shaft top, c.1950**

Here we can see lead miners at the top of the 300ft shaft at Oxclose Mine near Snitterton Hall. This was a very short-lived enterprise started in 1949 by Derbyshire Stone Ltd, who were recycling the spoil heaps of previous mining operations to recover fluorspar. With the discovery of an old shaft and an engine house, they took the decision to mine the fluorspar directly from underground. Unfortunately it soon transpired that it was an unprofitable exercise and the old works were abandoned again by the start of 1952.

**Castleton, entrance to Odin's Mine, 1866**

This print shows the entrance to Odin Mine, which was the main site for the extraction of Blue John, the famous variety of mineral known as fluorspar. This is a richly coloured mineral, predominantly blue or purple, the range of colouring of which is said to be due to chemical contamination by bitumen and iron. In the 18th century it started to become a highly sought-after commodity for its natural beauty, which could be enhanced in the hands of experienced craftsmen by skilful cutting, carving and polishing, to produce attractive ornaments of high quality.

### Darley Dale, Stancliffe stone quarries, *c.*1900

This impressive photograph shows a brief interruption to work taking place in one of the Stancliffe quarries. Men with pickaxes wait to get the signal to resume striking at the stone, while one man seems more concerned, not unreasonably, with keeping a large chain-bound block stable rather than posing for camera. The block is presumably being hoisted by the three-legged derrick into a position where the men would be able to work on it further. The derrick would also be used for loading stone into wagons, which travelled along railway tracks laid out all over the site.

### Darley Dale, Stancliffe workers, *c.*1925

This is a group of quarry workers standing by one of the railway tracks at Stancliffe Quarries. The quarries were worked for sandstone or gritstone from around 1840, and the quality of their products was immediately recognised. Intensive quarrying only took off after 1887, with mechanisation in the form of drag cranes, crushing plants and planing machines. Stone from Stancliffe found its way into a whole range of construction projects, including restoration stonework at the Houses of Parliament, the re-paving of Trafalgar Square and the making of crosses for the Commonwealth War Graves Commission.

**Matlock, Cawdor Quarry, c.1937**

This photograph of workmen must presumably have been taken before they started work, as they would have accumulated several layers of dust if it had been otherwise. They were working in the period before mechanisation had taken hold in the quarry, and it would certainly have been hard, heavy work. At the time when these men worked it, the stone would have been used for a variety purposes. Apart from use in building and construction, stone was an important component in the making of roads and commonly used as flux in the process of iron-smelting.

**Matlock, Cawdor Quarry, c.1946**

This photograph is supposed to show the first use of mechanised lorries, which did not take place until just after World War Two. Fred Gill, the quarry manager, and Alf Bunting wisely keep their distance as the stone is unloaded by the travelling derrick onto the lorry. Quarrying stopped there in the 1970s, although a stone-cutting plant remained in operation until the early 1990s. After several years of dereliction and discussion about its future, planning permission was eventually given for a new housing development and supermarket complex to go ahead on the old quarry site.

**Cromford, travelling crane at Dene Quarry, c.1950**

Work in the quarry, situated between the A6 and River Derwent, was started by local entrepreneur Herbert Hardy, who also began the DFS furniture chain. Although planning permission was difficult to obtain at first, the quality of the limestone obtained ensured that the small quarry prospered. Marketing literature of the time refers to the quarry's two trademarked types of marble, Hadene and Derbydene, which were used for interior and exterior linings, fireplace surrounds, memorials, tablets, sculpture and paving stones. The site is now owned by Pisani. The name of the man in front of the travelling crane is Don Harris.

**Hope, quarry works, c.1950**

Cows seem to have broken into the grounds of the quarry works, and it looks unlikely they are going to find much good grazing on this most inhospitable-looking industrial site, swirling with dust. The limestone at Hope has always been regarded as being stone of excellent quality, its principal uses being to provide lime for agricultural purposes and stone for roads. The site at Pindale to the south of the village has increased in size over time and continues to extend out even further under the ownership of Lafarge Cement.

**Castleton, lime burning kiln, *c.*1950**

Lime burning has always been a major industrial activity of the Peak District. Its main purpose for many centuries was to make lime for use in agriculture, where its alkaline properties helped to improve yields from land with acidic soils. The process involved the burning of limestone in kilns, using timber or coal as fuel. On the left is the archway which was part of the lime kiln at Black Rabbit off the Pindale Road, close to the quarries in Hope. Above the arch is the chimney shaft in which the limestone was burned.

**Birchover Quarries, masons at work, *c.*1950**

This photograph shows masons at work as they dress stone by hand. On the right we can see the round-headed mallet being raised, ready to strike. The other mason would seem to have a template of some sort in his hand, with its shadow falling on the stone block. The presence of the set-square rule shows how the mason has to ensure that the stone is cut and shaped to precisely the right dimensions. It is a highly skilled trade as well as a physically demanding one.

Ernest A. Smith, DCHQ005729

### Thornbridge Hall, stonemasons, c.1900

This photograph shows stonemasons working on Thornbridge Hall. The hall underwent extensive alterations and additions over the years 1896–1912, paid for by its wealthy owner, G.J. Marples. The amount of change Marples envisaged for the building meant that there were plenty of employment opportunities for skilled masons. The man in the bowler hat on the right is probably the head mason and holds a drawing of a stonework design. The other men in their caps, aprons and waistcoats hold a variety of appropriate tools, including rounded stone mallets.

Ernest A. Smith, DCHQ005741

### Thornbridge Hall, workmen at Woodlands, c.1904

Woodlands was an unusual building, performing the double function of providing recreation space for staff and estate workers of Thornbridge Hall and acting as a waiting room for passengers using the nearby railway station, which had been specially built for George Jobson Marples, a railway director and extremely rich businessman. This photograph was probably taken during its building in 1903–04 and is a fascinating shot, showing something of the social divides, that separate the smartly dressed young man striking a pose (possibly the architect), the site manager with his watch-chain and bowler hat, and the building labourers sitting on the rubble.

WOODBANK & MASSON MILL, MATLOCK BATH.

### Matlock Bath, Masson Mill, *c.*1900

This postcard shows a view of Masson Mill in its setting among the trees and cliffs of the Derwent Valley. The cotton-spinning mill was built in 1783 by Sir Richard Arkwright, making use of the river in a more effective way than his first mill just half a mile away. The mill continued in production for over 200 years, providing employment for many in the district. Unlike many industrial sites, it still retains some link with its past as it now houses a museum on cotton-spinning, the rest of the premises being used as a retail centre.

### Litton Mill interior, 1933

The photograph shows the interior of Litton Mill, with its machinery and some members of the staff and workforce. Litton was originally built by Ellis Needham in 1782 to make cotton. In the early days it became infamous for its use of child labour in appalling conditions. By the time this photograph was taken, people in general were no longer treated quite as badly. It even looks as if the bosses were prepared to let them put up Christmas decorations. The mill went the way of most of our manufacturing industry when it closed in the 1960s.

*Derby Museum and Art Gallery, DMAG000863*

**Bakewell, Lumford Mill, after burning down, 1868**
This photograph shows the ruins of the mill after it had burned down in 1868. It was then owned by the 7th Duke of Devonshire, who had bought it in 1860. It was ironic that he had done so, as one of his predecessors had been involved in litigation against the original owner, Sir Richard Arkwright, at the time of it being built. The mill was rebuilt by the Duke, who had obviously come to look on it as an asset. The mill was taken over in 1898 by the Dujardin-Planté Company, who used the site to make electric storage batteries.

**Bakewell, Lumford Mill, waterwheels, 1905**
This is actually a photographic copy of a painting by Elias Bancroft of the waterwheels at Lumford Mill. The cotton mill was originally built by Sir Richard Arkwright in 1777–78 to use power generated by the River Wye. The waterwheels pictured here had been introduced in 1827 and 1852. Made of cast iron, they measured 25ft and 21ft in diameter and lasted in working order for over 100 years before the gearing on the older wheel failed in 1955. The wheels were then replaced by a water turbine.

*Derby Museum and Art Gallery, DMAG000291*

**Matlock, Paton and Baldwin's Mill, *c.*1940**
This is a view of the mill belonging to the woollen goods manufacturers Paton and Baldwin. To the left is shown the original building on the site, which was named Victoria Hall. This had been built as a concert hall and pavilion for Matlock in 1896, aiming to provide entertainment for the guests in Smedley's Hydro nearby. It was, however, taken over at the start of World War One and turned into a factory making woollen goods for the war effort. After the conflict finished in 1918 it did not return to its original purpose, staying a factory.

**Matlock, Paton and Baldwin's Mill, carding machine, *c.*1985**
This is a shot of a worker maintaining a carding machine in the factory of Paton and Baldwin's Mill. Carding is the process by which woollen fibres are brushed, thinned out and aligned in preparation for spinning. The company Paton and Baldwin had taken over the mill in 1931, when it was known as Derwent Mill. Apart from a brief spell as a munitions factory in World War Two, it continued to manufacture woollen goods, but suffered the fate of most British manufacturing when economic conditions necessitated its closure in 1989.

### Castleton, Peak Cavern, rope-making, 1905

There used to be a whole community of rope-makers that had lived and worked within the cave since at least the 17th century, supplying rope for use in the lead mines in the area around Castleton. In the entrance were terraces along which each family worked their 'rope-walk', which meant literally walking back and forth, twisting and spinning strands of hemp into cords of rope as they went. In the photograph it is possible to make out a few levels of terracing, as well as the tall 'pulley poles' on which ropes were stretched with the help of large stones.

### Castleton, Peak Cavern, rope-making, 1818

This engraving shows it from inside the cavern, with the 'rope-walks' and the tall 'pulley poles' on which the rope was stretched using the weight of large stones. On the left hand side we can see one of the cottages that housed the workers and their dependants. Although gloomy, the arched entrance to Peak Cavern (also called 'The Devil's Arse') did provide shelter from the elements, so that workers could carry on regardless of the weather. With the decline of the lead mining industry in the late 19th century, however, rope-making was no longer a sustainable occupation at the site.

**Great Longstone, Thornhill and Sons Ltd, egg packing station, c.1960**

J. Thornhill and Sons Ltd were able to trace the history of their firm back to 1912 when John Thornhill set up as a poultry farmer. He expanded his business and established a nationally accredited egg-packing station at Great Longstone in 1930. Eggs were collected from producers within a 50-mile radius, quality-assessed and packed for dispatch. This was in the early days of mass-production techniques for farming, when it was unusual to use conveyor belts and automated processes to grade the size of eggs according to weight.

**Great Longstone, Thornhill and Sons Ltd, poultry processing, 1962**

We can see inside a Nissen hut, where young men are taking part in the unpleasant task of processing poultry. The poultry side of the firm's output had been somewhat overlooked by the egg-packing business, but it expanded rapidly after World War Two, particularly with regard to frozen poultry. By 1979 they were said to process nearly 300,000 oven-ready chickens per week, of which half were handled at Great Longstone. The plant closed, however, in 1989 after it had been taken over by J.P. Wood, with the loss of 300 jobs.

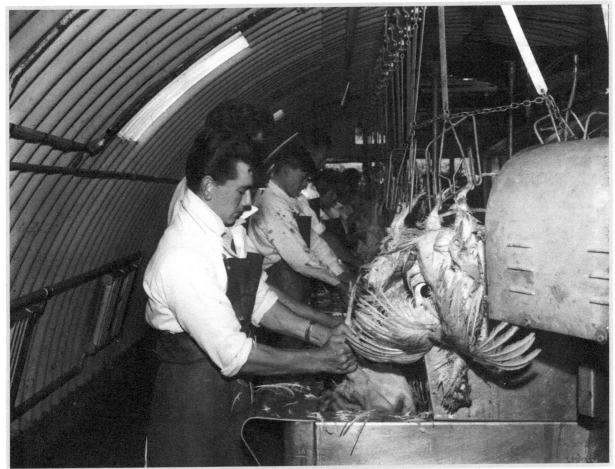

151

**Ashbourne, Nestlé factory, group photograph, 1925**

The railway lines and the wagons behind indicate that these were probably workmen who loaded the wagons for the distribution of Nestlé's condensed milk on the rail network. The factory on Clifton Road had been built for the Nestlé Anglo Swiss Condensed Milk Company in 1912 as one of its British centres for the product. It was a major employer in the town for many decades, but the factory was closed following the end of production in 2003. The site is now being redeveloped with the construction of affordable housing, business units and other local amenities.

**Ashbourne, Nestlé factory, tin shop staff, 1925**
This photograph shows a group of tin shop staff at the Nestlé factory. The factory made condensed milk, and these workers would have filled the tin cans in which the product was stored and preserved for distribution and sale. The female members of this section were known as the 'Tin Shop Girls', but this picture would indicate that there was a sizeable male presence there as well. The photograph was one of several taken on the occasion of the leaving of the manager, Mr Oscar Aubrey Rogers, who had managed the factory since its construction in 1912.

Mrs J. Gregory, DCHQS04794

### Calver Mill, cannery, c.1935

Pictured here are Stanley Gregory and an unknown female work colleague. They are working inside Calver Mill in Arthur Brayshaw's Cannery, whose core business revolved around the canning of peas. This was one of several pre-World War Two enterprises that people tried to establish there, after it closed down as a cotton-spinning factory in 1920. The site had seen its first mill built in 1778 and had gone on to be a successful operation after a catastrophic fire in 1802. This had not been enough to deter the mill-owners, who had set up a complex of buildings, recently developed for conversion into residential flats.

Published courtesy of the *Derby Evening Telegraph*, DCHQN06528

### Hartington, cheese factory, 1982

Cheese making was a traditional Peakland industry and there were several factories in the area in the late 19th century. There was, however, only one factory which survived into the modern era and this was the one at Hartington. It had originally been set up by the Duke of Devonshire in 1876, but was purchased in 1900 by a Leicestershire cheese-maker, Thomas Nuttall, who introduced the making of Stilton. It established a reputation for its quality and is now one of the few places that can officially produce Stilton. Here you can see an inspection of the racks of maturing cheese.

**Bakewell, J. Smith and Sons, printing works, 1925**

Joseph Smith and Sons had their premises on Rutland Square in Bakewell. *Kelly's Directory* of 1925 records them as 'stationers, printers, bookbinders, fancy goods depot & circulating library'. This is a view of the Composing Room, which is where the typeset blocks were put together so that they were ready to be inked and used in the printing press. Although it seems a long drawn-out process in these days of computerised printing technology, the well-honed skills of the typesetters and proof-readers meant that the end product had fewer typographical errors than would seem to be the norm today.

**Bakewell, Baker and Sons, sewing room, 1930**

This is a view of the sewing room of the clothing factory belonging to F.H. Baker and Sons of Granby Works on the Buxton Road. They had started a business making clothes for ladies in or around 1928 and seem to have lasted until the outbreak of World War Two. It looks as if they employed a relatively young female workforce, as all the girls seem to have the short haircuts that were so fashionable at the time. Note the scraps of textile on the floor that the girls have thrown behind them as they work.

**Ashbourne, Haycock's Clock Works interior, *c.*1910**
This is an unusual early photograph showing the inside of the clock works of William Haycock of Ashbourne. It shows a cramped but well-lit workshop, which was situated on Church Street. Ashbourne was once a centre of clock-making, but the Haycock business is now the only one still in existence. The firm was established in 1826, but has continued to carry on its highly skilled, hand-crafted traditions into the present day, providing a specialist service for the making of individual clocks, mechanical toys and precision engineered components.

**Ashbourne, Hans P. Hansen, photographer, *c.*1910**
This is a self portrait of Hans Peter Hansen, a photographer who had a studio in Ashbourne. Originally of Norwegian stock, he was actually born in Hull in 1868 but later moved to Ashbourne on getting married. Census returns show that he had originally been involved in the ship building industry, making iron plates, and that he also worked as a joiner and carpenter before turning to photography as a career. He later moved to Bramcote Hills near Nottingham, where he continued to practise his chosen profession. Several of his images are reproduced throughout this book.

### Rowsley, railway shed cleaners, *c.*1944

This photograph was taken during World War Two, when the manpower requirements of the war effort meant that women in the industrial workplace became the norm. The smartly dressed foreman, Jack Hibbs, stands with his shift crew, who all seem perfectly comfortable with their situation as shed cleaners and with each other.

Back row, left to right: Madge Wilmot, Rosie Mackley, Doris Holmes, Harriet Pinder, Pat Esplen, Doris Rudd, Daphne Evans, Mrs Evans, Ms Boden. Front row, E. Parker, Annie Hiden, Doris Wagner, O. Fearn, J. Hibbs, Edna Watken, Celia Middleton, Madge Elliot, E. Boam.

### Bradbourne, carpenter's house and backyard, *c.*1930

This photograph shows a row of cottages in Bradbourne, at the junction of the roads to Ashbourne, Hognaston and Brassington. At the end of the row, nearest the camera, is an old stone cottage and attached to the side of it is probably a workshop for the carpenter or joiner. In the yard, leaning on high fences, are a number of very long timbers, some of which stand taller than the cottage itself. This yard would later be the site of the King George V Memorial Hall, built some time after his death in 1936.

DCHQ0005673

Buxton Museum, DCBM2202204

# Transport and Travel

In the past the Peak District seemed somewhat inaccessible for many people. For the writer Daniel Defoe at the start of the 18th century, the difficulty of the terrain and the lack of proper roads had a particular influence, which helped to lead him towards his largely negative verdict on the area. There would, however, soon be developments that would remedy some of these deficiencies.

The road system was particularly weak, with poorly maintained surfaces. The development, however, of the turnpikes led to an improvement, as new roads were built and the tolls collected on them used to fund their maintenance. It would, however, be the onset of the railways that would open up the Peak District for all. People were now able to gain access to areas previously considered difficult to get to. This would be a process, of course, which the invention of the motor car would accelerate even more.

The images we have chosen mainly show the means by which people travelled about. There are the old stagecoaches, which used to be the only way to travel large distances, as well as smaller horse-drawn carriages, which were more useful for moving about locally, whether for work or leisure.

The onset of the motor car is reflected in the choices we have made. They are mostly of vintage or classic cars, showing a time when motoring was as much an adventure as a practical way of travelling from A to B. This is best reflected in the photograph of the fleet of Rolls-Royce cars, which were brought up to test their durability and reliability on the hilly terrain of the Peak District, in itself an indication of people's perception of the region in previous centuries.

There is also a selection of railway photographs, not only of the trains themselves, but also the structures linked with them, such as railway stations and the spectacular Monsal Dale Viaduct.

**Cromford, rider on horse, c.1870**
At the time this photograph was taken the easiest way to get around was on horse-back. Owning a horse for one's own private use was not a cheap option, requiring plenty of money to pay for stabling, feeding and a groom to take care of it. Here we can see James Arkwright astride a horse at his home, Willersley Castle. He would have had no problem in having the financial resources to cope with the situation, the Arkwrights of Willersley being one of the richest families in England in the early Victorian period.

Derby Library, DRBY007853

### Stanton Hall, pony and trap, c.1860

We can see two females all ready to set off in their pony and trap, but waiting for the photographer to do his work. They are pictured outside the entrance to the Thornhill family home, Stanton Hall in the village of Stanton in the Peak. The groom in the top hat has kept the pony standing on the spot, but has failed to keep its head still long enough for the required exposure time. This has not been such a problem for the gentleman casually leaning on one of the columns, who was probably the owner, William Pole Thornhill.

### Darley Dale, election horse and trap, 1910

This horse, 'Old Dick', is described as 'a staunch supporter of Lord Kerry'. He is out and about with his driver and trap, canvassing for support on behalf of Henry William Edmond Petty Fitzmaurice, aka the Earl of Kerry. He was standing as the Conservative and Unionist candidate in the West Derbyshire constituency during the general election campaign of December 1910. As voters were not able to vote for 'Old Dick' himself, they had to make do with Kerry, whom they successfully returned as MP even though the country as a whole ended up with a Liberal government, the last of its kind.

DCHQ002199

VOTE FOR KERRY

Jennifer Chadburn, DCHQ002182

### Matlock, three-horse dray on Smedley Street, c.1900

The dray has come to a stop, conveniently enough, outside the Crabtree pub on Smedley Street. The massive shire horses would have certainly appreciated the break, but they were not the ones making the decisions. On the dray is a drum of cable which, it is believed, is on its way to the depot for use in the Matlock tramway. Presumably, they have come the long way round to avoid the steep slopes of Matlock Bank. The only identified person is Alfred Ellis (third on the right), who used to work for the railway, along with his father, James.

**Ashbourne, horse and cart on country lane, c.1910**

This evocative photograph recalls a much earlier age, as a man wends his way along a country lane with his horse and cart. It is not, however, a timeless rural idyll, as the lane is quite muddy and would, no doubt, have been prone to get muddier still as the seasons passed. The telegraph poles by the left-hand hedgerow also indicate the presence of the modern world. The exact location of the lane is not known, other than it is somewhere around Ashbourne.

**Matlock Bath, horse-drawn carriages, c.1903**

The group of buildings here are the premises of H. Briddon's Posting Establishment, stabling 50 horses. Since 1866 this business had operated a fleet of different types of carriages to ferry inhabitants and visitors around, varying from four-horse brakes to dog-traps. The sign indicates that there were also public conveyances available to go to the main tourist sites, such as Haddon Hall, Chatsworth and Dovedale. These left at 10 o'clock each morning during the season. The premises were situated on the Derby Road but were later demolished to make way for the Pavilion, built in 1911.

**Baslow, coach, *c.*1900**

A coach to be drawn by four horses stands outside the Devonshire Arms at Goose Green. A large, well-dressed party stand or sit on the coach to have their photograph taken. It would have taken some time and effort to get everybody posed, and we can only hope, if only for the sake of the horses, that the coach did not set off with all the people still on it rather than in the other carriages available. If it had, those on top and at the rear would probably have cause to regret it.

**Hartington, coach and cart, 1906**

A coach and four horses with their passengers set off from outside the Devonshire Arms on the Market Place in Hartington, while a cart and a couple of horses await the return of their driver. This was a coaching inn built in the 17th century, which used to be known, appropriately enough for this particular picture, as the Waggon and Horses. The four-in-hand coach may have actually belonged to William Gretton, landlord of the nearby Charles Cotton Hotel and also a 'jobmaster', which the Oxford English Dictionary defines as a man 'who keeps a livery stable and lets out horses and carriages'.

**Bakewell, Rutland Square, *c.*1895**

Life moved at a very different pace in a market town like Bakewell before the advent of the motor car, although its time is not far away. The driver in the box-seat of the horse-drawn landau patiently waits for his employer to finish his business at the Sheffield and Rotherham Joint Stock Bank (now the Royal Bank of Scotland). In front of him stands a more prosaic pony and trap, whose owner is presumably inside the same establishment, seemingly unconcerned about any thought that they may no longer be there by the time he comes out.

**Buxton, stagecoach outside Milton's Head Hotel, *c.*1930**

At the time this photograph was taken, the stagecoach was definitely a thing of the past. The stagecoach had enjoyed its heyday in the time before the railways came, being the principal means by which those without recourse to private carriages travelled long distances in and out of the Peak District. In 1823 there were five coaches that called in daily at Buxton on their way to and from Manchester, Sheffield, Derby, Macclesfield and London. This particular one was said to have been the last London to Brighton stagecoach, evidently being a tourist-type attraction rather than seriously lost en route.

Mrs J. Gregory, DCHQS04809

**Calver Sough Toll Bar, c.1878**

This toll bar was set up on the main Chesterfield-Hernstone Lane Head Turnpike Road. The gates would be opened by the toll bar keeper on receipt of the appropriate amount of money for the type of horse-drawn vehicle concerned, such as a coach, carriage or wagon. On the side of the keeper's house above the gates can be seen a large board with the table of fees, most of which were supposed to be spent on the upkeep of the road. This photograph was probably taken in around 1878, when the turnpike trust that took care of the road was wound up.

**Winter, making of road, c.1900**

The laying of a new road surface would not normally attract a crowd today, but it was obviously an event for the inhabitants of Winster at that time. No doubt the steam roller would have made the biggest impression on the locals, hopefully not literally. Asphalting had usually been restricted to the larger cities before that time, so to have had it in a rural village would have been something of a coup. The widespread use of the safety bicycle and the introduction of motorised vehicles had led to increasing calls for smoother, better road surfaces in rural areas as well.

DCHQ00648

**Baslow Bridge toll-shelter,** *c.*1950
A curious boy peers into the small, stone-built shelter which used to house a watchman at the eastern end of the bridge at Baslow. The watchman would look out of his circular window to see any carts approaching and then come out to take the payment of toll-money for the vehicles to go over the bridge. It is known that tolls were collected at Baslow as early as 1500. The shelter came to be known in the early 20th century as Mother Brady's Cottage, named after an Irish beggarwoman who stayed in the area and slept rough in there.

**Grindleford, cyclists, _c._1900**

Here we can see two lady cyclists who have paused to be photographed on the road out of Grindleford, with a fine view of the Derwent valley looking over towards Hathersage. As a relatively cheap form of transport, bicycling opened up the countryside for all classes of society. Women, in particular, took advantage of the freedom the newly invented safety bicycles gave them to get out and about. In spite of some initial lampooning by male critics and fears raised on highly dubious medical grounds, the sight of ladies cycling along became so common that it hardly excited any comment whatsoever.

**Buxton, vehicles outside the Cat and Fiddle, _c._1915**

Different types of vehicle stand outside the Cat and Fiddle on Axe Edge, about five miles west of Buxton. On the left is a carriage containing several people awaiting its horse, in the middle are a motorcycle and sidecar, and on the right is the motorised bus that ran between Buxton and Macclesfield. The bus was obviously in no hurry to be getting along, as a man leans on the front wheel drawing on his cigarette. The inn was built in about 1800 to provide refreshments for those travelling on the new turnpike road, and later became a popular tourist destination in its own right.

Published courtesy of the *Buxton Advertiser*, DCHP000584

**Buxton, motorcycle team, 1966**

These three young men, Norman Eyre, David Rowland and Mick Andrews, had been taking part as a team in the Scottish Six-Day Motorcycle Trial. David Rowland, however, had a trial of a different sort, being called on to give evidence at Derby Assizes in a murder case. Having started the race in the belief that he might not actually be needed, he found out that his presence was required after all, so he had to withdraw. At the time he and the team had looked on course to win. As it was, Mick Andrews came third, and Norman Eyre finished 12th overall.

**Ashbourne, car on Church Street, *c.*1910**

The appearance of a car on the streets of Ashbourne at this time would not have been a total novelty, even though the ownership of cars was still largely restricted to the wealthy or the enthusiastic amateur. The car has a chauffeur in his peaked cap at the wheel, hiding somewhat behind the windscreen framework. On the side of the vehicle is the spare wheel, absolutely essential for any journey then as tyre technology was not as advanced as it is now and the condition of most roads made punctures the norm rather than the exception.

**Buxton, fleet of Rolls-Royce cars, 1909**

This photograph shows a real piece of motoring history, with a small fleet of world-famous Silver Ghost cars. These particular cars, registered under the index marks CH R, were among the first vehicles made at the Derby factory, which had opened in 1908. The cars underwent rigorous testing for reliability in the Peak District, where the weather, steep gradients and tough road conditions would prove whether they really were up to the job. That they did so can be gauged by the fact that the Silver Ghost shortly gained the accolade of being 'the best car in the world'.

**Taddington, car outside George Hotel, c.1910**

The impressive motor car stands outside the George Hotel at Taddington, as the driver and owner lets his pride and joy be photographed. In this case we know who he was, a Mr Belton of Ravenstor, Millers Dale. He was an entrepreneur who patented Virol, a mixture of cod liver oil and malt, which was sold nationwide in chemists' shops. At this time such a car would have been a fair indicator of the owner's social and financial standing, particularly of the upwardly mobile variety. The landlord, Mr Fox, stands close by in admiration with his wife and family.

**Wensley, Peak Trial, classic car, 1959**

In April 1959 owners of classic cars gathered to take part in the Peak Trial, which involved taking their machines rallying on various courses in the Peak District. This photograph was taken on the stretch at Clough Wood near the site of Mill Close Mine. We can see how tough the event must have been, as a sports car is put through its paces up an improbably steep gradient. The event was popular throughout the 1950s, but was later amalgamated with the Edinburgh Trials to enable its continuation.

167

**Baslow Bridge, motor accident, 1915**

This extraordinary photograph shows the aftermath of an accident involving a charabanc full of holiday makers from Sheffield. It was reported that the accident came about when the steering gear got locked with the accelerator pedal as the vehicle rounded the sharp bend onto the bridge, which caused it to shoot forward into the stonework. Fortunately, the axle box came into contact with a stone large enough to prevent the charabanc from tumbling down into the river. The passengers showed great calm and presence of mind as it teetered on the edge, and everybody was able to get out safely.

**Two Dales, caravan site, c.1960**

Among the millions of visitors who travel to the Peak District there are many people who bring their caravans and stay on the several sites dotted throughout the area. Caravans are always capable of inducing Jeremy Clarkson-style rants when people get stuck in a queue behind one, but this would have happened much more regularly at the time of this photograph, when the cars pulling them did not have the power even quite small vehicles possess today. This particular site was set up at Two Dales in Darley Dale.

**Matlock, Allen family taxi,** *c.*1912
This photograph shows a taxi about to be driven by William Allen, as it stands outside the former United Methodist Chapel in Imperial Road. The driver sits in a surprisingly spacious compartment of his own with a fixed roof, while his passengers seem to have less room and only a folding canopy for cover. We can get a good look at some of its features, such as the luggage hold on the roof and the mounting of the spare wheel. There also appears to be a speaking horn behind the driver, with which he could communicate with his passengers.

**Hathersage, car and charabanc at Surprise View,** *c.*1920
Surprise View is to be found at Millstone Edge on the way to Sheffield on the A6187. This bend in the road actually took some making, as the labourers employed by the Sparrowpit Turnpike Trust in 1825 had to cut their way through a great mass of rock to open up the route. In this photograph the surprise is not so much the view as the fact that the charabanc has no shadow. It also looks in the wrong position for taking a bend and out of scale with regard to the car approaching it.

Mr C.R. Taylor, DCHQ005695

**Matlock, gas-powered charabanc, 1917**

As we consider the alternatives to petrol-powered vehicles these days, it is interesting to see there had been other experiments with alternative forms of energy. During World War One supplies of petrol were prioritised for the war effort, so efforts were made to convert non-essential vehicles to run on gas. The storage container for the gas might be considered somewhat primitive by some, being only a large canvas bag attached to the roof, but it did apparently work. The charabanc is parked on Crown Square in the centre of Matlock town, outside Fearn's bicycle shop.

DCHQ005433

**Via Gellia, charabanc, 1912**

This was an early version of the deluxe football team coach, a Belsize charabanc arranged for Matlock Thursday football team to take them off for a game in Ashbourne. It's a bit of squeeze, especially as there are also some supporters there, not something which would be tolerated today. The chap at the front with the chequered top hat and distinctive moustache was the team mascot, 'Toddy Clayton'. Other people included Harry Toplis (driver), Walter Bowler (courier), Mrs J. Platts, Miss M. Platts, E. Knight, W. Eldridge, T. Anderson, P. Statham, P. Webster, C. Mitchell, G. Nesbitt, G. Buckley and G. Gregory.

**Cromford, coach at High Peak Junction, c.1966**

With the demise of the railway linking Derby and Manchester, the main form of public transport for many towns on its route became the bus service. This photograph shows a Leyland Leopard single deck coach with Willowbrook bodywork, which was used on the newly introduced service from Derby to Buxton, travelling up and down the A6. The service was operated by the Trent Motor Traction Company, the leading fleet operator serving the East Midlands, which had been founded in 1913, its first task being to provide staff transport for a country estate at Ashbourne.

**Ashbourne, day-trippers at the station, c.1955**

People, including several families, throng the platform at Ashbourne Station in the summer sunshine. They are waiting for a day trip or excursion train, which was a popular form of transport. In the days before most families had the resources to own a car and before the railway network was drastically cut back by the Beeching report, the excursion train was a good way for people to travel beyond their local area and enjoy themselves on a day out. People from Stoke-on-Trent and the Potteries, in particular, took advantage of the chance to come this way to visit Ashbourne and the Dove Valley.

Grindleford Station.

**Grindleford, horse-drawn carriages at station, *c*.1905**

On this postcard several horse-drawn carriages stand outside the station, waiting for day-trippers to emerge. The building of the railway line to Grindleford and other villages in the Hope Valley helped to open up the area for visitors and tourists to explore. In this particular case, the sender of the postcard did not particularly enjoy his time, as the message on the back says that it was a 'very uncomfortable day today, roads all soft and splashy'. It was, however, in the middle of February, so it could have been expected to a degree.

**Grindleford, Totley Railway Tunnel, *c*.1911**

Grindleford Station stands at one end of the Totley Railway Tunnel on the Dore-Chinley line. Although this tunnel was a major engineering feat, its building is an achievement that is comparatvely little known. It is no less than 3½ miles long, making it the longest complete railway tunnel in England. It took five hard years to build between 1888 and 1893 and many difficulties were encountered in that time, including particularly severe water drainage problems. The *Manchester Guardian* reported that 'every man seemed to possess the miraculous power of Moses, for whenever a rock was struck, water sprang out of it'.

GRINDLEFORD STATION.

### Millers Dale Railway Station, c.1900

This is a view of the railway station at Millers Dale with part of the village below it. The River Wye flows below the houses and the stone viaduct, along which the Midland Railway line ran between Manchester and Derby. This photograph must date from before 1905, when a second viaduct was built to avoid the congestion which frequently happened there. Also visible is the Railway Inn, at the bottom of the steep roadway. In front of it are a pony and trap, which might have been used to ferry grateful passengers and their luggage to and from the station.

### Cromford Railway Station, c.1907

The station was constructed as part of the Manchester, Buxton, Matlock and Midlands Junction Railway in 1849, but was later taken over by the Midland Railway as part of the main line linking Derby and Manchester. The station boasts a couple of surprising French chateau-style buildings, a stationmaster's villa and a platform waiting-room with a pointed roof flourish, attributed to G.H. Stokes, the son-in-law of Sir Joseph Paxton and dated around 1860. Although the buildings remained, the station lost some of its lustre after the link with Manchester was broken when the line north of Matlock was closed in 1968.

Mrs Radford, DCHQ000479

**Cromford and High Peak Railway, accident, 1937**

Over the course of this railway's history there were several accidents, often involving engines that failed to make the steep inclines and ran back down the track. Usually they resulted in little more than damage to wagons and the inconvenience of clearing up the track. In this particular case, however, the accident proved more serious, having fatal consequences. While working up speed to climb the Hopton incline, the train derailed as the track curved round and toppled over the embankment. Although quite near the bottom of the incline, the fall was far enough, unfortunately, to result in the driver's death.

**Longcliffe, Cromford and High Peak Railway, 1957**

A steam engine is taking on water from tenders on a ramp at Longcliffe. The type of engine is known as a Saddletank, where the water tank is curved over the boiler, something well brought out by the angle of this photograph. The Cromford and High Peak Railway was constructed in 1830 and covered a distance of 33 miles. It was principally used for the transport of minerals and goods to and from the Cromford Canal at High Peak Junction and the Peak Forest Canal at Whaley Bridge.

W.I. Brighouse, DCHQ000879

## Buxton, train passing through Ashwood Dale, 1907

On this postcard we can see a Midland railway passenger train on its way towards Buxton. It is in Ashwood Dale near Lovers Leap, just south-east of the town. This line, the Midland Railway Rowsley and Buxton Branch, was opened in 1862, extending journeys up from Derby and the south to link through to Manchester. Although much of the branch-line was closed in 1968, this particular stretch remained in use to provide freight access to and from limestone quarries in the area. To the right of the tracks are the River Wye and the A6 road, all running in parallel along this narrow dale.

## Monsal Dale Viaduct, c.1924

This viaduct was built in 1863 as part of the Midland Railway Buxton–Rowsley branch line. It provoked an angry response from John Ruskin, the Victorian man of letters, who deplored the destruction of the valley, so that 'every fool in Buxton can be at Bakewell in half-an-hour, and every fool in Bakewell at Buxton'. No doubt he would have been pleased when the line was closed in 1968, and later opened up as a trail for walkers. The viaduct certainly had an environmental impact and changed the landscape, but people could argue that it actually added something.

**Matlock, tram for Rockside Hydro, c.1910**

Matlock, for a time, had a cable tramway, which served a very useful purpose in ferrying people up and down the steep hillside of Matlock Bank. The tramway opened in 1893, several years after it had been first proposed. It was particularly valuable for visitors staying at the hydropathic establishments, one of which was the Rockside Hydro, close to the last stop at the top. The tramway, unfortunately, ran at a great loss, and the decision was taken to close it down in 1927, something that successive generations of residents, workers and visitors have had good cause to regret ever since.

**Matlock, trams passing on the Bank, *c.*1910**
Here a couple of trams travel past each other at the cross-roads between Bank Road and Smedley Street. This is the point where the Cable Tramway temporarily switched from a single to double track, allowing more than one tram to operate on the tramway at the same time. Tram No.2 is heading down towards Crown Square, while No.3 is making its way up towards the top. It looks as if several people are about to get off shortly, some of whom are likely to be heading for Smedley's Hydro or the shops on the left.

**Cromford Canal, barge, 1980**
The Cromford Canal was built between 1789 and 1794, starting at the wharf serving Cromford Mill and running for 17 miles to the Erewash Canal at Langley Mill. Principally designed to serve the purposes of industry, its original builders and owners would have been amazed at its present usage as a site for recreational use and wildlife preservation. In this particular photograph enthusiasts crowd a barge at Meadows Wharf ready to set off along the canal. They are members of the Cromford Canal Society, which had done so much to restore it from the derelict state precipitated by its closure in 1944.

177

Published courtesy of the *Derbyshire Times*. DCHQ006585

**Derwent Dam, 'Dambusters' Return', 1981**
An Avro Lancaster plane flies past in spectacular fashion during celebrations of the part played by the reservoirs of Howden and Derwent in preparation for the famous 'Dambuster Raids' during World War Two. The reservoirs were used over a six-week period by 617 Squadron to practise low-level flying techniques and the dropping of the 'bouncing bombs', as designed by the inventor and engineer Barnes Wallis (born in Ripley, Derbyshire). They were chosen, particularly the Derwent, on account of the similarities of terrain to one of the target dams in the Rühr valley, the Sorpe.

# VISITORS AND TOURISTS

The Peak District is today heavily dependent on the tourist trade. It provides thousands of jobs and brings millions of pounds into the local economy, without which the region might struggle to remain a viable economic unit. It is not difficult to see why visitors are attracted here: beautiful countryside, with a variety of landscapes shaped by the disparate forces of nature and man, and a cultural heritage embracing everything from the stately homes of the rich and powerful to the old cottages of humble lead-mining villagers.

It is interesting to note, therefore, that this appreciation is a comparatively modern phenomenon. Hard as it might be to believe, people tried to avoid coming into the Peak District unless they had to. To some the countryside here was the opposite of beautiful, more 'a waste and a howling wilderness' in the words of Daniel Defoe, and a comparative backwater, devoid of civilisation.

There has, however, been a marked change in perception over the last 250 years, as people have learned to appreciate nature as it is, even the wastes and wildernesses, and to recognise that civilisation can exist outside the metropolis. As people grew richer and had greater opportunities to enjoy leisure activities, so the urge to travel and see new horizons increased. It became easier to actually get here, particularly following the introduction of the railways, improvements in road networks and the invention of the motor car.

We have tried to show images that reflect the range of tourist and visitor activity in the past: the growth of Buxton, Matlock and Matlock Bath as spa or health resorts, the appreciation of impressive landscapes in the dales, the discovery of marvels in the natural world around us and the visiting of historic sites, whether they be the great stately houses or prehistoric monuments.

**Haddon Hall, visit of Belgian volunteers, 1867**
In 1867 a troop of Belgian volunteers visited the Peak District. They were originally formed to help Maximilian of Habsburg become Emperor of Mexico, but were then in England as part of a goodwill exchange between military volunteers. While they were in London, they heard the news that Maximilian had been betrayed to Mexican rebels and executed. In spite of the bad news, the Belgians carried out their intention to come up north and were duly fêted wherever they went, including at Haddon Hall. Although some of the men here are in uniform, they may actually just be the band that accompanied them.

**Haddon Hall, group of tourists on terrace steps, *c.*1880**

Haddon Hall became one of the main tourist destinations of the Peak District in the late 18th century. A guidebook of 1838 refers to it as 'a noble mansion of the olden time, which is believed to be the only perfect edifice of the kind now remaining in England'. In many ways the Hall complemented and contrasted with the splendours of Chatsworth, offering for some a more atmospheric experience with a real sense of history. The group here have rested on the steps of the small but beautiful terraced garden, whose basic design dates from the early 18th century.

Mr D. Roberts, DCHQ006596

**Harthill, stone circle at Harthill Moor, *c.*1950**

Here a man stands looking at the Nine Stones Close circle, otherwise known as the Grey Ladies, on Harthill Moor. There are now only four stones standing, although another one was later used as a gatepost in a nearby wall. Originally part of a stone circle 45ft in diameter, the stones measure between 4ft and 7ft in height, making them the tallest in Derbyshire. The name 'Grey Ladies' comes from the legend that they are supposed to dance at midnight, although the extension of the licensing hours means they can be seen to do so at any time.

C. Eric Brown, DCHQ006597

**Bakewell, view from Castle Hill, c.1906**

The sender of the card, one Rachel Harris, comments: 'This is a most lovely place. It is so hot we can't walk about much in the middle of the day.' Bakewell is one of the oldest towns in the area, with origins in Anglo-Saxon times when it came to prominence with the building of a military stronghold against the Vikings nearby. A castle was later constructed during the Norman period, but only one made out of wood. Very little evidence of it now remains, apart from the name of the hill, from where you get a fine view over the town.

**Buxton, the Old Hall Hotel and the Crescent Hotel, c.1916**

The Old Hall was built in 1573 by the Earl of Shrewsbury, and received several visits from Mary, Queen of Scots to take the cure, during the time when he was literally her gaoler. The hotel itself was erected later to cater for other, less politically dangerous, visitors wanting to improve their health. Behind it in the picture is the Crescent, which was built for the 5th Duke of Devonshire as part of a conscious attempt to improve Buxton and replicate the success of Bath as a fashionable spa town.

**Buxton, dining room at the Crescent Hotel, c.1910**
Here we can see some of the opulence expected by visitors staying at what was then the grandest hotel in Buxton. The Crescent had been built between 1780 and 1784 to designs by John Carr, who was heavily influenced in his neo-classical interiors by the great architect Robert Adam. There are several country houses that would have quibbled over the 'finest example of Adam decoration in the kingdom' tag (not least because it isn't actually by Adam!), but there is no doubt it would have been an impressive place to have done one's dining.

**Buxton, St Anne's Well, c.1909**
This free outdoor pump was provided for the benefit of residents and visitors in 1894. Here we can see a small terrier taking advantage of the opportunity to take on some water. The caption reads 'Canine Instinct, taking the drinking cure at the well of St Anne, Buxton.' The emphasis on its curative properties has diminished over time, but the growing awareness of the need to avoid dehydration has meant that Buxton water is still a highly valued commodity, bottled and sold under the leading brand name of Buxton Water.

### Buxton, St Anne's Well, interior, *c.* 1912

This sunken marble basin was situated in St Anne's Well, which was the name given to the renovated and enlarged Pump Room in 1912. It received its water from a newly-found spring source, coming up through the holes in its base. The postcard has a somewhat alarming caption, referring to a 'constant flow of radioactive thermal mineral water', a tag not likely to attract many customers today. People were, in fact, trying to link Buxton water with what were seen as the positive benefits of the recently discovered element of radium, before its adverse long-term health effects became apparent.

### Buxton, Thermal Baths douche massage, *c.* 1912

Many different treatments were available in Buxton. This particular type was known as the Buxton douche massage, which involved lying in a shallow copper bath, being hosed with water at 35–38°C and receiving a massage. The temperature of the water was gradually lowered until the patient could no longer take the cold. It usually took between 10 and 15 minutes, after which he or she would be wrapped in towels and allowed to rest. Other forms of treatment visitors could try included peat baths, facial massages, mud packs, sand baths, Jacuzzis and, for the really brave, the electro-water bath.

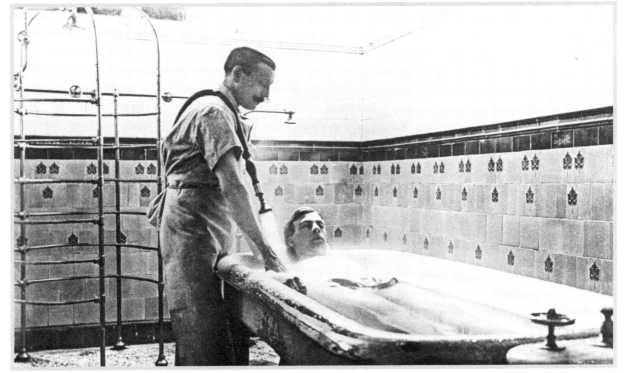

**Buxton, Devonshire Hospital Dome, interior, 1935**

The spectacular dome was built between 1879 and 1881, as part of the improvements designed by the architect R.R. Duke for the Devonshire Hospital. In spite of initial opposition to the proposed cost, the construction of the dome was to prove an architectural triumph. With a diameter of 164ft, it was the largest unsupported dome in the world at the time and attracted tourists to see it in its own right. After the hospital closed in 2000, the building was incorporated into the Buxton campus of the University of Derby.

**Buxton, bathchair in the Pleasure Gardens, c.1910**

Bathchairs were immensely useful for visitors who came to the town for health reasons and found it difficult to move around. Here we can see a gentleman, with his two ladies, being led on a tour around the Pleasure Gardens. The bathchair looks very comfortable, with a padded leather seat raised so that the occupant could enjoy a conversation without being talked down to, and there is a hood in case it rains. The man pulling it was George Pyle, one of the bathchairmen who often travelled long distances, hauling their clients along.

**Buxton, the Broad Walk,** *c.*1908

The Broad Walk was a development of substantial residences, planned primarily to attract the gentry and the wealthy, and strictly controlled by the Devonshire estate as regards their architectural style and use. Several Italianate villas were constructed between 1861 and 1876 and did become highly desirable properties as private lodging houses or hotels. As its name would suggest, it became a highly popular place for tourists and local people to promenade along, being free of traffic and very close to the attractions of the Pleasure Gardens.

**Matlock Bath, man and lady on Lovers' Walks,** *c.*1910

The couple here are on one of the paths that makes up the network known as Lovers' Walks, which are on the eastern bank of the River Derwent, opposite the town's shops, houses and other buildings. Sheltered by the steep rock face and overhanging trees next to the river, it is indeed an ideal place for a pleasant leisurely stroll. Genuine lovers, however, hoping for a more secluded spot and a bit of privacy, might find they are in for some disappointment, as there never seems to be any shortage of people choosing to travel along those paths.

**Matlock Bath, South Parade, 1888**
Tourists stroll along the South Parade during the height of the season, something they would be well-advised not to do now, as the road is part of the busy A6. A guide of 1906 states that day-trippers would make up the majority of visitors, who would arrive by train in the morning, immediately set off for Haddon Hall or Chatsworth in charabancs, and return to eat a big tea. They would then feed the golden carp in the fishpond, listen to the band, maybe even dance a little, and then head off home by the early evening train.

**Matlock Bath, Old Bath Hotel, 1811**
Matlock Bath started to attract visitors to take the waters after the discovery of a hot spring in 1694. This soon led to a demand for accommodation to house them, which was partly met by the building of this hotel, which actually incorporated the spring itself within its premises. The town's reputation as a fashionable spa resort soon grew. It attracted a clientele made up of the wealthy or the upper class, most of whom stayed here, including the poet Lord Byron. It would later be radically rebuilt and renamed the Royal, in recognition of the status of some of its customers.

**Matlock Bath, Woodbank guesthouse, c.1910**

Visitors who stayed for more than a day could lodge at one of the several guest houses which dot the hills in Matlock Bath, well above the river and the bustle of the shops and traffic. This sizeable house, Woodbank, was originally built by the manager of Masson Mill, but was later used as a boarding house. It was to be the residence of the card-writer for a week, who had not quite appreciated how hilly the area was going to be. He wrote, 'Wharfedale looked so strenuous that we decided against it. This bids fair to be worse.'

**Matlock Bath, Royal Museum petrifying well, c.1920**

One of the distinctive attractions of Matlock Bath used to be the petrifying well. This was the largest and most popular of such wells, where a variety of objects were continuously sprayed with mineral-rich water as it left the spring. The spray deposited tiny speckles of lime, which over a year accumulated as a crust, so much so that it looked as if the objects had been turned into stone. In the picture, closer examination will reveal a policeman's helmet, cups and saucers, baskets of fruit, rolled-up umbrellas, tobacco pipes, porcelain figurines, shoes and egg cups with real eggs.

**Matlock, Chesterfield Grammar School field trip, *c.*1896**

This must be one of the earliest examples of a school outing in the Peak District on record, with the boys and teachers being taken out into the countryside around Matlock. The progressive headmaster behind it was James Mansell, in post from 1894 to 1921, who sits in profile to the left of centre. He has brought along his wife Sarah, their young son Ralph (both sitting in the front row, to the left) and their daughter Eva (at the front on the extreme right), who would end up marrying the head boy, Frederick 'Gus' Sharpe.

**Matlock, Smedley's Hydro, dance in ballroom, *c.*1920**

Although Smedley's was a hydropathic establishment, offering some visitors the opportunity to receive medical treatment for their ailments, it had a wide range of facilities in-house for others just to enjoy themselves. Advertising material called these particular people the 'Pleasure Seekers'. Those facilities included extensive gardens and grounds for walking, tennis courts, a bowling green, putting lawns and a billiard room. There was also a Winter Garden, where people could exercise and enjoy other forms of recreation, including the regular dances which used to take place on its specially designed 'Spring Dancing Floor'.

**Matlock, Smedley's Hydro, social event, c.1930**

This photograph shows a party where there is a bit of role-reversal going on. The people sitting down are members of staff, who are about to be waited on by customers. It does not look like it is a forced occasion in any way, with plenty of drink, which may be indicative of the more informal atmosphere that gradually took hold after the death of its founder, John Smedley. This is taking place during the inter-war period, when the hydro was rather more of a hotel than a medical establishment offering treatment, apparently very popular with ex-colonial army officers.

**Smedley's Hydro, staff in kitchen, c.1910**

This shows the staff enjoying a good laugh while they are having a tea-break in the kitchen. For a long time after its invention people did not generally express any sort of emotion in photography. The equipment and its technology required people to stay absolutely still for several seconds, so most people adopted rather stiff and formal poses. The introduction, however, of more portable equipment, in particular the Box Brownie, meant people posed in a much more relaxed fashion and could even be caught right off their guard, as this spontaneous shot would seem to indicate.

**Monsal Dale, church outing, c.1900**

Here we can see members of the Matlock Bank Wesleyan Methodist Church, who have taken a day out to travel up and enjoy an outing in Monsal Dale. They are lounging on the rustic wooden footbridge at Upperdale, which was close to the railway station serving the dale. It is possible they came on the train over the railway aqueduct, whose building caused Ruskin such pain. The bridge is situated at the point where the Wye valley opens out and has a softer character as the river flows south down towards Bakewell.

**Cromford, Black Rocks, Victorian visitors, c.1870**

At Cromford, on the road up towards Wirksworth, there is an impressive outcrop of gritstone rock soaring above a wooded hillside, known as the Black Rocks. They live up to their name, contrasting with the white limestone cliffs of Matlock Dale a mile or two northwards. It might look as if our Victorian visitors with their heavy clothing might have struggled to reach such heights, but access is comparatively easy. One gentleman has been a little braver and gone to the edge of one of the pinnacles, called the Promontory, to take in the splendid views around about.

**Cromford, camping at Castle Top Farm, 1936**
This photograph is in an album made by Alfie Johnson, extolling the virtues of the camping life at Castle Top Farm. In somewhat overwrought prose he writes: 'What do they know of it, they who have never trodden the crisp heather or battled with the breezes on the hill-tops? What do they know of it, they who have never stood at a tent door, and looked out across the valley at nightfall, seeing the twinkling lights appear in the villages, or in lonely farmhouse windows? As long as I live the hills must call me, and as long as I live I will answer them.'

TISSINGTON SPIRES. DOVEDALE.

**Tissington Spires, c.1905**
The sender of this postcard, a Walter Brown, was writing to a friend, a Miss Savage of Stockport, in August 1905, summing up the attractions of the Peak District. 'We have had a very pleasant, quiet, peaceful time – nothing exciting but very soothing, very refreshing. It is coming to an end all too soon. The scenery is most delightful, not flat like tedious old Cheshire but beautifully diversified with its uplands and dales, its grassy hills and swift streams.' Hopefully, the recipient did not take the adverse comment on her native county too much to heart.

James Alexander Heyworth, DCAV002591

### Dovedale, boy on donkey, 1928

Donkeys used to be a regular attraction for many years in Dovedale, just like they used to be at the seaside. They acquired here something of a reputation for being a bit 'skittish' and 'giddying about' very quickly. In this case, the rider of the donkey is six-year-old James Heyworth of Belper, who was to experience much greater speeds than any donkey could manage. He went on to become an acclaimed squadron leader for Bomber Command during World War Two and then the chief test pilot for Rolls-Royce.

### Dovedale, road and traffic, c.1930

Here we can see that Dovedale was quite busy in summer, even in the 1930s. Cars make their way along the lane leading to Thorpe, careful to avoid the pedestrians, some of whom have their water bottles much as now, in earthenware jugs slung over their shoulders rather than plastic containers. The popularity of the valley as a tourist destination owes much to the works of the celebrated angler Izaak Walton and the poet Charles Cotton, who eulogised its beauty. Both would have been staggered to find out that in the future Dovedale would attract a million visitors a year.

### Stepping stones at Dovedale, c.1960

Hikers and a dog take the time-honoured walk across the stepping stones over towards the other side of the River Dove. They are regarded as the usual entrance to the scenic part of the Dove valley and the point where walkers start their journeys northwards. Following the river upstream through the gorge, they would pass a whole series of impressive geological features, landmarks which have acquired evocatively romantic names, such as the Twelve Apostles, Tissington Spires, Reynard's Cave, Lion's Head Rock, Ilam Rock, Pickering Tor and Dove Holes.

**Lathkill Dale, works outing at Conksbury Bridge, c.1935**
The Peak District has often been the location for works outings. Here we can see a group of men from the firm of Haslam and Newton Ltd, of Derby, which used to specialise in the manufacture of refrigeration equipment. The men have come up to enjoy the fresh and healthy air of the beautiful Lathkill Dale and, as if to prove it, have stopped for a good old smoke by a wall at Conksbury Bridge. The names of the men are (standing, left to right): 'Pert' Walker, Jack 'Drummer' Lowe, Ron Balderston and Harry Moore and (squatting) Richard Armitage and Mr Turner.

**Birchover, Robin Hood's Stride, young men, 1948**
Two hikers stand on Robin Hood's Stride on Stanton Moor, a twin-towered crag of millstone grit, left isolated by the erosion of rocks around them. The link to the legendary outlaw is, alas, totally spurious, although the site is still a subject of historical debate. The discovery of supposed rock art, set within the context of several mounds and monuments in the close vicinity, has resulted in it being linked with prehistoric religious practice. The two young men pictured here, 'Bob' and 'Tom', aka John Tomlinson, were workers at Shipley Hall Colliery opencast coal site.

**Castleton, inside Speedwell Cavern, *c*.1910**
The journey by boat in the unique underground canal system became one of the more unusual tourist attractions in the area. The opportunity to enjoy this experience came about as a consequence of the unsuccessful attempt to mine ore deep in the hillside, which ended after 11 years of largely fruitless digging in the late 18th century. Here we can see the landing stage, from where visitors are transported by guides who push the boat with their hands and legs along the tunnel walls and ceiling into the heart of the cavern, where they can explore its many fascinating geological features.

**Castleton, entrance to Speedwell Cavern, 1909**
The entrance is to be found at the foot of Winnats Pass, half a mile west of the village of Castleton. Access to the cavern is now made by walking down a flight of 104 stone steps rather than being lowered down in a large bucket, which is what used to happen to the lead miners over 200 years ago. Tourists seem always to have been able to enjoy access to the cavern, even in the years when mining took place there. Increasing curiosity during the 19th century about the natural world, including its geology, cemented its reputation as a tourist attraction.

**Wheston Cross, 1858**
In 1858 the then-amateur photographer Richard Keene and three friends undertook a six-day ramble over the hills and dales of the Peak District. They took a particular interest in the area's history, and several photographs were taken of churches, crosses and other ancient monuments. This cross at Wheston is generally thought to date from the 15th century and marked the boundary of the Royal Forest. Although weathered, it is finely carved, with a representation of the Crucifixion at the top. Unfortunately, they were not able to photograph the other side, which showed the Virgin Mary and Child, because of 'obstacles'.

**Rowsley, Peacock Hotel, 1858**

Keene and his friends came up from Derby on the train and got off at Rowsley, briefly passing the renowned Peacock Hotel. The people shown may be two of his companions on the trip. The man sitting on the camshaft of a horse-drawn cart may possibly be Mr Tillett, who had charge of his own smaller cart, which was specially made to take all the photographic apparatus. He seems to have taken on the sole burden of lugging it about himself, so he may not have enjoyed the ramble quite as much as his pals.

Derby Library, DCHQ006595

**Haddon Hall, courtyard entrance to great hall, *c.*1876**
Although Keene was not able to get to Haddon Hall on the 1858 trip, because they ran out of time, it was a place he was to visit several times after he took up photography as a professional career. Haddon Hall was no longer inhabited by its owners, the Dukes of Rutland, but it did not quite suffer the destruction or general neglect of many other mediaeval castles. It survived as the proper image of what a castle should look like, with battlements, towers and courtyards and even had a romantic legend attached to it, involving the elopement of Dorothy Vernon with John Manners.

Derby Library, DCHQ0006589

### Eyam Cross, 1858

Keene and his companions particularly enjoyed their stay at Eyam, including their egg and bacon breakfasts. While seeing the sights associated with the celebrated outbreak of plague in the village, time was also taken in the churchyard to photograph the cross, which dates as far back as the ninth century, if not earlier. Here we see Keene himself, reading a book seemingly oblivious to the fine Scandinavian-type scrollwork carved on the sides of the cross and the images of angels on the headstone. This photograph was taken by his close friend, J.A. Warwick.

### Hope, general view, c.1905

The writing at the bottom of this postcard says 'This is sweet little place, very quiet, right away from everywhere.' The sender of the card, 'Doll', was staying at Park View Cottage in the village of Hope, and she wrote in 1905 to her friend in Gloucestershire: 'We are having a lovely time here, in the midst of such beautiful country, I never thought the Peak District was so lovely. We have nice rooms, & everything we could possibly wish for. Yesterday we had a beautiful day at Chatsworth.'

DCHQ0006541

**Chatsworth, view of west façade, *c.*1920**

No chapter on visitors and tourists in the Peak District would be complete without some references to Chatsworth House, regularly accorded by many organisations the accolade of being the country's best stately home. This timeless view of the classical architecture in the midst of a magnificent landscape shows the home of the Dukes of Devonshire, and their duchesses of course, in its all its glory. Add in the sumptuous interiors, the art treasures and the splendid gardens and it is not hard to see why well over half a million visitors a year are attracted here.

**Chatsworth, drawing by G.I. Morant, 1839**

Ever since the house was built in the late 17th century it has been open for people to see. In the 18th century the housekeepers had instructions to show people around on request. In 1844 it was noted that the Duke 'allows all persons whatsoever to see the mansion and grounds every day of the year' and that 'the humblest individual is not only shown the whole, but the Duke has expressly ordered the waterworks to be played for everyone without exception'. This attitude was commended as being 'in the true spirit of great wealth and enlightened liberality'.

W.H. Brighouse, DCFQ003410

**Edensor, Chatsworth Estate Office, c.1960**

The importance which the Dukes of Devonshire placed on access for tourists can be seen in this building, which was designed by the noted architect Joseph Pickford. It was originally built in 1778 as an inn to accommodate the sightseers who travelled to visit the house. It is now the Estate Office, which serves as a hub for the business activities of the house and its associated shops and farms. It is an important part of the enterprise, which means Chatsworth is currently regarded as the ideal business model for the running of a stately home and its estate.

# WICKED WEATHER

As everybody is talking about climate change and coming to terms with the impending catastrophe of global warming, it seemed appropriate to put in a section about weather in the Peak District. There is, of course, weather going on all the time, but we have chosen pictures that show its influence and effects at particular places and on particular occasions.

Snow figures highly in the selection of photographs, whereas the sun hardly seems to make an appearance at all. This might perhaps be doing the Peak District a disservice, as even the gloomiest resident would have to admit that the sun shines far more than the snow falls. We have, however, concentrated on the consequences of the times when it does snow.

There is something about snow that adds a certain excitement to our lives, particularly when we are young. It can also be beautiful as a number of our photographs will hopefully show. As we get older and our bones creakier, the combination of snow and ice becomes a less attractive proposition. The bitterly cold winters of 1946–47 and 1962–63 live long in the memory for many people here at the time, when the snow outstayed its welcome even for those who enjoyed all it had to offer.

Among older people, there is a definite consensus that the winters are milder and less snowy than they used to be. If this is due to the effects of global warming, and as the trend for less snow continues, such wintry scenes really may become a thing of the past for the inhabitants of the Peak District.

If it is the case that there is less snow in the future, it is possible that it might mean more rain instead. We have chosen here a few examples where excessive rain has caused flooding in the past to places along the rivers Derwent and Wye with startling impact.

**Buxton, the Great Snowstorm, 1933**

The Peak District was hit by what was called the Great Snowstorm on the afternoon of Friday 24 February. This storm would last for 50 hours until the afternoon of Sunday 26 February. Disruption to the region was severe, as roads became impassable, telephone wires came down and villages were cut off. Even attempts to airlift relief supplies to the village of Flash proved impossible. Great efforts were made by council workers to clear away snow from the roads and pavements, and we can see the end result of using footpath-ploughs on the High Street.

*Published courtesy of the Buxton Advertiser, DCHQ006574*

**Buxton, Goyt Valley relief expedition, 1933**

In the aftermath of the snowstorm of 24–26 February, Messrs Burgon Ltd had to resort to horses to get food and supplies through to workmen building reservoirs in the Goyt Valley, who were cut off and short of food. A party of seven horses and riders, including Lee Bussey of the High Peak Riding School and George Critchlow, set off from the store in Spring Gardens. They encountered terrible conditions, going through snow waist-deep for over a mile at one stage, but managed to get through. As luck would have it, they arrived at the same time as a relief lorry from Whaley Bridge.

*Pat Smith, DCHQ000643*

**Sterndale Moor, making deliveries, 1933**

The snowstorm that affected the Buxton area meant that some places were cut off for a number of days. It was initially difficult to get supplies through, but local communities eventually received them. Here, men are delivering provisions to the cottages at Sterndale Moor. These were company cottages occupied by the families of workmen who were employed by Imperial Chemical Industries Limited (better known as ICI) in the limestone quarries close by.

**Buxton, snowbound lorry, 1933**

People are finding it difficult, but at least they are moving about here. The lorry, however, has got stuck halfway up Terrace Road. Supposed to deliver his cargo of timber from a Manchester saw mill to the yard of building merchants Messrs J.W. Swain Ltd, the driver found himself assailed by the onset of blizzard conditions. Although only a few hundred yards from his destination, he wisely decided to pull up and let the weather take its course. It would, however, be about a week before he was finally able to deliver his load.

**Farley, deep snow drift, 1947**

This gives the best indication of the scale of the winter of 1947. During the month of February and early March snow fell on almost every day, and there were equally severe frosts and freezing conditions. In terms of weather records this would prove to be the heaviest winter for snowfall since 1814. The photographer has stopped his car at Shining Well near Farley Hill to get out and take a picture of his vehicle dwarfed by sheer cliffs of snow.

**Farley, workmen clearing snow, 1947**
Workmen are trying to clear snow off one of the roads near Flash Dam north of Farley. They are actually employees of John W.M. Wildgoose and Sons Ltd, builders and contractors, who have undertaken the task of clearing access along one of the more out-of-the-way routes, while mechanical and other types of snow-ploughs were in use on major roads. It would have been hard work, probably made harder if the clearing they made was closed up by more drifting soon afterwards.

**Aston near Hope, snow clearing, 1947**
Here we can see the work of the inhabitants of Aston, who have banded together with their shovels and spades to clear a way out of their small village on the northern side of the Hope Valley. No doubt they would have had to do this on many occasions, but this was probably the worst winter any of them would have experienced. They are clearing the road near Aston Hall Farm. The man nearest the camera is known to be Tom Sidwell.

Buxton Museum, DCBM000029

**Fairfield Common, snow clearing, 1947**

The bus returning to Buxton has become stranded during one of the heavy snowfalls and been abandoned. Apparently, drifts on the common were up to 10ft deep, and we can see how some of the snow has drifted up to cover the windows on the driver's side. The driver of the bulldozer is in position to clear a way round the bus for other vehicles to get through, although the winter was such that it would have probably not have been long before he had to do it all over again.

DCHP000140

**Buxton, horse-pulled snowplough, *c.*1920**

In the days before the mechanisation of snow clearing, the streets of Buxton saw the use of horse-powered snowploughs. A team of at least three shire-horses (they could number four) are being led along Dale Road with a plough attached behind them, pushing the snow to the sides as they move forward. A man walks behind to keep everything steadily in check. Unlikely as it seems, someone did once slip and fall in front of the plough and was killed as it went over him.

**Buxton, snow falling on dairy cart, 1965**
Although it has started to snow on Dale Road, milk deliveries are still taking place. The horse drawing the cart was called 'Tom', and he is being steered along by Mr R. Mosley. Both were working for Morten's Dairy, who were still using the same form of transport as in 1907, which can be seen on page 102 of this book. This photograph was taken not long before the business was actually sold. It went on to became part of Express Dairy, and horses like Tom would have been replaced by motorised milk floats.

**Cromford, railway track in snow, early 20th century**
Trying to keep transport communications open is an obvious objective whenever there are any substantial snowfalls. In this case the tracks of the Cromford and High Peak Railway have been cleared so that trains are able to proceed again through the narrow gap in the rocks. This is one of a number of photographs where those inspecting the lines have posed in front of the train for the camera.

**Peak Dale, damage to cables, 1941**

Here we can see the damage caused by ice loading on power cables. The steel structure of the pylon has crumpled spectacularly under the weight of ice on the cables. It happened along the electricity line from Buxton to Glossop and obviously affected local communities. It was, however, during wartime, when hardships were met with stoical acceptance. The local newspaper reports on a concert at Dove Holes to raise funds to provide gifts for local men serving in the armed forces still taking place in lamplight.

**Chatsworth, frozen cascade, 1942**
The winter of 1942 was one of a series of bad winters which hit during World War Two. We can see how cold it was by the freezing of water in mid-air, as it cascaded down the Sowter Stone waterfall at Chatsworth. Sowter Stone is a natural outcrop of rock in Stand Wood to the east of the house. It was modified to take a waterfall in the 1830s, being one of the features introduced by the great gardener and designer Sir Joseph Paxton.

### Cromford, mill wheel frozen up, 1963

The winter of 1962–63 is generally regarded as the coldest since 1740. From just before Christmas to the beginning of March, the whole country was under a blanket of snow, but it was the cold that really struck home. Temperatures rarely seemed to rise above freezing, and there were extensive air frosts nearly every night. We can see how it affected the water wheel at Cromford, as the water has congealed into ice. The wheel is to be found at the pond on Water Lane, which was put in to help provide a steady supply of water to power Cromford Mill.

Published courtesy of the Buxton Advertiser, DCHP000236

**Peak Dale, home under snow, 1963**

This is an example of how people can get trapped inside their homes when the snow starts to drift in the Peak District. Here Mr and Mrs Garner stand outside their terraced house on Upper End, which felt the full brunt of the weather during the infamous winter of 1963. In spite of its name Peak Dale is actually a village that lies on top of the moorland just north of Buxton and sits exposed to the elements. Around it are the limestone quarries that give the majority of families their livelihood.

**Buxton, snow house, 1898**

Although the country as a whole did not experience much in the way of snowfall in 1898, Buxton seems to have lived up to its reputation of having a micro-climate of its own, providing enough of the white stuff to build this house. It must be about 10ft high, with quite a large entrance, which an adult can enter without having to bend too much. A child stands inside, dwarfed by the structure. It stood outside Buxton station, so we can assume that the men responsible were involved with the railway and obviously not too over-worked.

**Buxton, tobogganing on the Manchester Road, *c.*1906**

It is hard to imagine the council letting people toboggan down a main road these days, but life moved at a very different pace then. Manchester Road was a particularly popular place to go tobogganing, as it curved and swept down at just the right angle into town. Here we can see a young couple who have gone by the Clarendon Hotel, in front of quite a crowd of spectators, hoping for a soft landing at the end. Unfortunately, there were times when there wasn't one, and a number of accidents meant that tobogganing was later discouraged there.

**Buxton, skating on lake, _c._1950**

Skaters are out on the lake in the Pavilion Gardens in the Macclesfield Road area. This lake was intended as a boating lake in the summer months, but it was designed in such a way that the water levels could be lowered to a foot or so in winter, so that it could be frozen over and used safely as a skating rink. For many years it proved immensely popular with the people of the town, as well as visitors, whom the town authorities tried their best to attract in winter.

**Buxton, ladies curling, _c._1910**

Curling took place at one of three rinks in the Pavilion Gardens. The rinks were made out of a shallow pond which could be frozen over during the winter and used for ice-skating and curling. There had actually been a Buxton Curling Club since 1895, with the rinks at the Pavilion Gardens being opened in 1906. It would seem to be the same lady in both shots, getting down into the right position to send down a stone on the left, and waiting to start sweeping it towards its target on the right, while wearing a splendidly wide flat cap.

### Buxton, gentlemen curling, c.1910

As well as the rinks at Pavilion Gardens, there were smaller ones which took advantage of the freezing conditions that the town frequently experienced. It was another example of the playing of winter sports in Buxton, something which the town authorities liked to encourage and promote at that time. This particular rink was to be found at the rear of the Grove Hotel. The Grove itself was once a fashionable coffee house in the 18th century, then a coaching inn, before establishing its position as a leading hotel of the locality.

### Ashbourne, Lady Cockayne's Walk, c.1910

Lady Cockayne's Walk was a tree-lined path which skirted the grounds of Ashbourne Hall (part of which is now the site of Ashbourne Library). It was named after a female member of the family that used to own the hall, until it was sold by the poet Sir Aston Cockayne in the 17th century. The walkway was also known as the Dark Walk. Unfortunately, the chance of seeing this view would not last long after this photograph was taken, as the walk was destroyed just before World War One, when the estate was broken up and the lands sold.

Buxton, snow-swept Cat and Fiddle Inn, with dog, 1919

At an altitude of 1,690ft above sea level the Cat and Fiddle for a long time held the claim of being the highest pub in England. Although no longer able to hold that particular title, which has gone to a hostelry in Yorkshire, this did not stop it remaining a tourist destination in its own right. The high altitude and exposed position in the moorlands above Buxton does lend it a certain distinction, but it also means that the inn is at the mercy of bad weather, as this particular image, taken on 28 April 1919, shows.

Sparrowpit, winter scene, 1925

This picture shows the small village of Sparrowpit. This is a view looking eastwards, showing most of the houses, which line up along one side of the road from Chapel-en-le-Frith. Situated at a place where a number of routes through the Peak District cross, it is a village which is severely exposed to the elements. The snow here is not thick on the ground, but the dark, menacing sky seems to indicate that the situation is probably about to change for the worse on this February day.

215

### Castleton, Peveril Castle, 1936

This particular picture was taken by an individual who lived locally and regularly photographed the castle. Here he has captured it during the snows of December 1936. We can see the impressive stone keep, which stands proud almost to its original height. It dominates the landscape above Castleton and Cave Dale, with its impregnable defensive position at the top of perpendicular cliffs. William Peveril, an illegitimate son of William the Conqueror, built the castle that bears his name in 1080. It was originally a wooden structure but was subsequently fortified with stone however, it had fallen into disuse by the time of the Tudors.

### Buxton, view of Pavilion Gardens in snow, c.1940

This view shows the River Wye in the Pavilion Gardens in winter. These grounds had originally been part of the old Hall Gardens, which had been set up by the 5th Duke of Devonshire so that townsfolk and visitors could enjoy the option of taking some healthy walks in pleasant surroundings. Trees were planted, rustic bridges constructed and walkways laid out. Although they were initially maintained by the Devonshire Estate, the gardens were later enclosed to be linked with the new Winter Pavilion, which was built in 1870.

216

**Fairfield, view of snow, 1944**

This is a general view from Corbar over towards Fairfield, on the north-east outskirts of Buxton. The snow is slowly going away, but not before leaving a stunning landscape to photograph. The areas where the snow has not melted contrast with those where it has remained to create a network of geometric patterns in the landscape. This picture was taken in March 1944, during one of the very harsh winters which predominated in the 1940s and added to the sense of struggle that people were experiencing at the time.

**Monsal Dale, snowy landscape, c.1945**

After the initial, physical exhilaration and experience from being out in it, and in spite of the trouble and inconvenience it causes others, we are also able to appreciate just how beautiful snow can be. Here, the photographer has gone out walking and come across this view of an isolated farmstead in Monsal Dale set against a background of a snowy hillside and bare, individual trees. No doubt, this would be attractive at any time of year, but the snow does add something to the scene.

**King Sterndale Church, in snowscape, 1962**

A fine winter scene, as the parish church shows itself through a row of trees. The church was built in 1847 in the early English style to serve the community at King Sterndale, a secluded village three miles east of Buxton. The village was originally part of the manor and forest of the Peak, which used to be directly owned by the Crown, which accounts for the first part of its name. The name Sterndale derives from Old English, literally meaning 'valley with stony ground'.

**Buxton, cloudy sky over moorland, late 19th century**

This picture showing clouds over moorland near the Cat and Fiddle Inn gives a good impression of the landscape around the area west of Buxton, which can look particularly bleak when the weather turns nasty, which is quite common there. This particular image has survived on an original glass negative plate. Although it has done well to remain intact, a problem for all glass negatives, it has suffered quite a lot of damage over time, with spots, scratches and even thumb prints.

**Matlock Bath, South Parade, slush on road, *c.*1903**
The snow has started to melt, and it is a bleak, dreary day, which somehow always seems worse in Matlock Bath, where the steep hillsides and the mists around them just add to the gloom. No pedestrians have felt like braving the weather, but two carts and their horses make their way through the slush up South Parade. The photograph was taken in front of the Fishpond pub. Along the left-hand side little has changed, but on the right-hand side the buildings were taken down several years ago.

**Matlock, flood on Bakewell Road, *c.*1907**
Flooding was a common occurrence in Matlock for many years. Here a horse splashes through the water on Bakewell Road, as the smartly-dressed driver looks down to see where the wheels of his Landau carriage are actually going. To his side a couple look back down the road, while behind him a lady sits back, not particularly enjoying her trip by the looks of it. They are passing the shop of William Furniss, who was principally a cab and coach proprietor, but who also operated little sidelines as a hairdresser and tobacconist.

Mr M. Arkle, DCHQ003968

### Matlock Green, flooding, 1931

Floods struck again in September 1931 after a night of rainstorms. Water streamed down from the hills, first hitting houses which would never have been considered under threat, and then flowing on into the Bentley Brook. This brook soon burst its banks, causing a flash flood in Matlock Green. Although the water subsided almost immediately, it was only a brief reprieve, as the River Derwent followed suit in overflowing. The crisis point would now seem to have passed, as a couple of women survey the scene, and a lady, boy and family dog hazard a trip to Francis Taylor's fruit shop.

### Matlock, flooding in Crown Square, 1965

The worst outbreak of flooding to hit Matlock is generally acknowledged to be the one that occurred on 9 and 10 December 1965. The combination of snow thawing in the Peak District hills and heavy rain over a sustained period was made worse by the fact that it happened at a time when the reservoirs further up the Derwent Valley were already brim full from the autumn. The bus spent a night stranded in Crown Square after its occupants had been rescued, and its position had actually been shifted by the strength of the water-flow to the one seen in the photograph.

Published courtesy of the *Derbyshire Times*, DCHQ003980

### Matlock Bath, car in tree, 1965

This extraordinary image shows the huge impact that the flood waters had in December 1965. This vehicle had been left in a car park at Matlock Bath, but such was the power of the water that it was lifted up and deposited further down the river. The death of a man at Bentley Brook and the damage caused to homes, shops, roads and pavements led to calls for action. It was, however, only in the 1980s that flood prevention works actually took place to avoid any repetition of such scenes.

### Darley Dale, flooding, 1941

This is a view of the area around Darley Bridge during the floods of February 1941. This is a stretch of the River Derwent where flooding occurs relatively frequently. On this occasion the flooding was caused by a rapid thaw of the snow that had accumulated up on the hills, which must have been very heavy indeed as there was no accompanying rainfall to swell the river. This picture has perfectly captured the moment when the trees are mirrored in the still waters.

### Bakewell, flooding of the River Wye, 1984

Swift thaws and torrential downpours soon afterwards led to severe flooding of the River Wye on Thursday 9 February 1984. On this occasion swift thinking prevented a number of homes in the Granby district from being inundated. Peter Melland erected an improvised barrier of boards along the pavement, when he discovered the water levels critically high. With the help of neighbours Walter Hallows and Brian Betney, the temporary barrier was strengthened with sandbags to withstand further incursions. As we can see, the water already seems quite close to the top of the wall as it curves round, but nothing worse happened.

### Buxton Pop Festival, crowd in the rain, 1973

Just as the Glastonbury Festival is now associated with rain and mud, one of its lesser known predecessors, the Buxton Pop Festival, invariably invoked the same weather conditions. The festival of July 1973 almost descended into total chaos. With the arrival of the then-notorious Hell's Angels and their invasion of the stage to avoid the mud, the headline act, Chuck Berry, found himself performing in an intimidating atmosphere. The star's speedy retreat was followed by more shenanigans and ructions, involving dodgy promoters and stroppy bands. Needless to say, all is remembered now with nostalgic affection for the good old days.

### Chatsworth, wind damage, 1962

During the night of 15 and 16 February 1962 a hurricane-force wind swept across the Peak District, leaving a trail of destruction in its wake. Trees were felled in Chatsworth Park by the wind, and we can see here how some fell on the old mill there. The damage was so severe that the building was written off and never repaired. Its ruins are still there today and can be seen by people who drive through Chatsworth Park or walk from the Calton Lees car park on their way to visit the house on the other side of the river.

### Derwent, church re-appearing during drought, 1947

With the building of the Ladybower Reservoir completed, Derwent Church held its last service in 1943. The church was then taken down, apart from the tower, which was left standing as a memorial to the demolished village. The waters gradually rose over the next couple of years, submerging everything except the tower. Over the summer of 1947 there was a drought which caused the water levels to fall so much that people were able to revisit the site. As the tower was no longer considered safe after its immersion, the decision was taken to demolish it, which duly happened on 15 December.

223

**Ashbourne, Recreation Ground paddling pool, 1955**
This is just a photograph to show that the weather in the Peak District is not always so bad. It is on the occasion of the opening of the paddling pool, which took place in July 1955. Parents and grandparents look on as their charges test the water. The boys have leapt forward to take advantage of the fountain spraying them with water, while the girls stand back (with one gallant exception). Several girls have already taken the precaution of tucking up their dresses in such a way as to not show their underwear.